PRAISES FOR BROKEN NO MORE

"Imagine being lifted above your troubles by an all-powerful King -- a King who brings you an abundance of love, grace, hope and peace, and who heals your life in its broken places. Is such transformation possible? Yes! And your journey can begin today with the eternal truths in this amazing story and life-changing book. *Broken No More* is a treasure that will help you and your family live in victory over despair, and triumph over darkness!"

Michael Lynberg
Author of *The Gift of Giving* and *Make Each Day Your Masterpiece*

"Scripture teaches us that if we boast we should only "boast in our own weakness" that it may be perfectly clear that the source of whatever is praiseworthy in our life is God. Mary Ann's courage to use her life as the canvas to minister God's love and grace is a breath-taking example of this idea in action. Not only do we read about Mary Ann and God, but we are able to read ourselves into her story and come away with many of her life lessons as our own. A great book and a great minister in the making!"

Bryan James
Senior Pastor
Monterey Church

"Maryann's book has helped me realize that there's more to the story than flesh and blood. There is a God whose hand is over our lives redeeming everything that we may think is too small or even too far gone to salvage. But, there is an enemy who encourages us to think that those things are indeed too small for a mighty God; too soiled even for Him to wash clean. Maryann is transparent, and her story will convince you to see with new eyes what redemption really means."

Jeff and Heather Owen
Tenth Avenue North

"We all know people who have survived traumatic backgrounds but every now then you get the privilege of meeting an exceptional person who has not just patched up the wounds of their life but has allowed these seemingly destructive events to catapult them to an inspirational level of influence and service to others. My friend Maryann is such a person and this intimate and compelling account of her journey to wholeness and Christ centered victory will have you not only cheering for her but for yourself and others as well."

Russell and Christine Fragar
Hillsong Australia

Broken No More
I Am Because He Is

MARYANN MCMELLON

WESTBOW
PRESS
A DIVISION OF THOMAS NELSON

WestBow Press books may be ordered through booksellers or by contacting:

WestBow Press
A Division of Thomas Nelson
1663 Liberty Drive
Bloomington, IN 47403
www.westbowpress.com
1-(866) 928-1240

ISBN: 978-1-4497-6267-4 (hc)
ISBN: 978-1-4497-6268-1 (sc)
ISBN: 978-1-4497-6269-8 (e)
Library of Congress Control Number: 2012914374

Printed in the United States of America

WestBow Press rev. date: 08/20/2012

This book is dedicated to the Lord of heaven, my Father, my Prince, the One who came to rescue me from brokenness so that I would be broken no more. Thank you, my Jesus, for the work you have begun in me. May I bring you glory. To my husband, Michael: can you believe God would bring us this far? I love you more today, and I am proud to be your bride. Thank you for working so hard and supporting this ministry! To my children, Ashley and Jacob, future war heroes: lift up your swords and remember that the battle may sometimes be fierce but you have already won! Thank you for being patient while mommy wrote her book. I love you both and I am so proud of you.

CONTENTS

FOREWORD

*May He crown you with the honor of knowing
that you fought always to set the captives free*

The fingerprints of God are all around us, and you'll find them if you just know what to look for. These fingerprints are evidence of God's ability to pull a miracle out of a disaster. And I guess that is the greatest hope we all have in God. We can know that no matter how dire, how ugly, or how hopeless our situation is, there is always the master architect who is gently smiling and saying, "Hey, why don't you let me take over. I can fix this."

There is one story in the Bible that, for me, is the most emotionally charging. You'll find it at the end of the first chapter of the book of Mark. It is only 6 verses long. A man with a terminal disease...destined to die in pain, alone and deformed, runs and kneels before Jesus. The man knows exactly who he is kneeling in front of. He knows that only Jesus can heal his leprosy. He begs Jesus, "If you are willing, you can heal me and make me clean." I love this next part. Without any parable, or a sermon about how sinful mankind is, or a lecture for the crowd to hear, the Bible says that Jesus was "moved with compassion" (I believe He was smiling through watery eyes too), when he said "I am willing. Be healed."

Those three words, "I am willing" always run like electricity through me. Are those not the words that best summarize Jesus' life? He was willing to leave his heavenly throne and come to earth. He was willing to be the ultimate sacrifice in our place. And He is willing to step into your life even now.

The book you hold is a story of a woman who bears those same fingerprints of the Master. In her transparency you'll get a raw, front-row view of a crushing life that was all but extinguished. I won't spoil the ending, but know that it ends better than it begins. However, I hope you see more than just a story. I hope you look deeper...look for the fingerprints... look for the hands that heal, the heart that breaks for His child, and the Master who said, "I am willing". Because in the end, it is not someone else's story that matters to you... it is your story. Find Him. Run to Him. Kneel before Him. Ask Him in. I promise you, He is willing.

Maryann, my wife, my love, my best friend, thank you for letting me write this foreword in your book. I am honored to be your husband, and to share this life along side you. You inspire me. I am not sure why God chose me to be the lucky guy that gets to walk this world with you, but I'm sure glad He did. I thank God for the purposes and plans He has. May your life always magnify Jesus. May your words always reflect His greatness. May He crown you with the honor of knowing that you fought always to set the captives free.

I love you,
-Michael

PREFACE

He heals the brokenhearted and
binds up their wounds.

—Ps. 147:3

*D*ear Father,

Happy Father's Day! I have been yours and you have been mine for eleven years now! Today marks the day I gave my life to you, and to think this year the anniversary fell on Father's Day! I used to visit a grave to place flowers over a tombstone on Father's Day, feeling much sorrow over losing my Dad and always envious of my friends who still had fathers. But I am no longer fatherless! You, Father, rescued me from darkness, and how I was once so afraid of that dark!

I celebrate my eleventh year as your daughter. I think about how I was adopted into your family, and as I write, I can't help but to cry. I am consumed by you. Your love overwhelms me; in fact, I can barely see the keyboard because I am sitting here completely overwhelmed by you! You are the love of my life. I never truly felt love or knew perfect love until that day, the day I met you! Oh how you love me! You died for me, and yet the grave could not hold you or keep you from me. You are my rescuer and my deliverer! No one knows me like you, and yet you still came for me.

On this Father's Day, I want to write a book in hopes that I can bring you glory. I am no skilled writer—I hardly made it through high school, as you know—but I trust that you will take my small portion in writing this book and multiply it. If you, Father, have brought me this far, what's a book? Please anoint me to tell my story and make me brave enough to be transparent. Apart from you, I am not skilled enough to write a sentence without a grammatical mishap! So this book is a test of faith to the greatest degree! My desire is to tell the world about a man who came to my rescue, a man who went to war for me, a man who possesses the power that conquers death, hell, and the grave, and the man who saved my life. Broken I was, but today because of Jesus, I am broken no more!

ACKNOWLEDGMENTS

*L*ord, am I really doing this? Am I writing the acknowledgment section of a book? I don't know where to begin. How can I put into words what you brought me through and how I feel about you? Can a book do you justice? Words are not enough to describe you. I am grateful that I am your child and that you love me. You are my treasure. Thank you for loving me back to wholeness, for healing my wounds, and setting me free. May I be a reflection of your glory for all to see. I love you so much.

To my husband, Michael, a man who looked past my wounded self and saw something much more, thank you for your support and encouragement. You believed in me, and I could not have asked for a finer husband and friend. Thank you for your commitment to Christ and for showing me what a godly husband and marriage look like. We sure have learned a lot together, haven't we? It is an honor to be your wife. Eleven years of marriage, and I love you more today than ever before. Thank you for joining me to serve God's kingdom and for being a great war hero in our family. Not only are you a great husband, but you are an amazing father. I am blessed! Please hurry home from Afghanistan!

I am overwhelmed with gratefulness for our two children, Ashley and Jacob. I am so proud of you and praise God that He permitted me to be your mom. I am also honored to be your teacher. You both amaze me daily, and I am blessed to watch you grow up and develop into God's warriors for the kingdom. I need only watch you, and you minister to me. God uses you both to speak to me. As for this book, I know my story may be hard for you to understand, but my past is what brought mommy to her Savior. And I will always be grateful for that. What a joy to be your mom. You are one of the greatest blessings in all my life. I cannot wait to see God's calling for your lives. No doubt, we will war together! We already have!

I must acknowledge my sister, Kriste, and my mom, Linda. Our home was not perfect, and life has been hard. But if that is what led us all to Christ, I rejoice in all of it! Mom, I am sorry for what you have endured these past few years. However, I am grateful to have you in my life again. Thank you for choosing life when you heard about your pregnancy. God had a plan. I trust that the Lord will continue to transform your life and your mind. Kriste, I am sorry for the way you were treated growing up, but I am blessed to have a twin. God knew we would need one another in this journey. The Lord has a plan for your life, and He will bring it to fruition. Never give up! I love you. There will be a day, Kriste, when you and I speak to the masses side by side, and as my pastor said, "Imagine what the double anointing could do to the Devil." Sounds like a plan to me, twin!

To Mom McMellon and Dad McMellon, thank you for accepting me as a daughter-in-law without requiring a background check. You accepted me regardless of my past, and never once did I feel judged. You have also encouraged me in my calling, and I am grateful. Thank you mostly for that son of yours and how you raised him. I love you both.

To my sister in Christ, Elaine James, you encouraged me to write this book from the day we met. You were the first ever to speak words of encouragement to write. So here it is finally. Thank you for believing in me and thank you for all your direction in life. Lord knows I need it!

Monterey Church, thank you for permitting me to counsel the flock. My counseling ministry began with you, and I praise God for your leadership, Pastor Bryan, and thank you for saying yes to a student fresh out of grad school and yes to a woman you knew was a mess! What great faith, PBJ! Your leadership at Monterey Church helped pave the way for BrokenNoMore Counseling. You will always hold a place in our hearts, and we are so thankful for you and Elaine as well as the entire body of Christ at Monterey Church, our family.

I must also give thanks to every client who sat in counseling with me or Skyped from afar. You have all touched me profoundly. I have seen the hand of God in your lives! I have had the privilege of watching a handful of you receive Christ in session. How great is our God! As I was counseling you, you counseled me. I see a war hero in every one of you. I have been honored and blessed to be at your side. May we continue to war against Satan together. We may be wounded in the fight, out of breath, but in the end, we will all hear "Well done, good and faithful servant, well done!" Never give up! I am so proud of you, and hearing your stories about how Christ saved your marriages and set you free has been one of the greatest privileges and honors I could ever ask for. I love you all. May God continue to use your lives for His glory. That is why you are here!

To all my sisters in Christ, thank you for your prayers and support. You have all helped me greatly. I love your hugs! Your prayers have lifted me up and carried me in hard times. And to my brothers in Christ, thank you for putting up with me! You have all been a voice in my life, a loud one!

And finally, a very special thanks to Pastor David and Jo Ann Baird, You sent BrokenNoMore to Latin America and helped publish this manuscript. You have been a huge influence in my life and family. Jo Ann, you are a woman of great wisdom and I admire you. I love you both, and thank you for believing in me. I praise God for Life Church. Thank you for encouraging me and allowing me to be part of the call.

INTRODUCTION

It is good to give thanks to the Lord,
to sing praises to the Most High.

—Ps. 92:1

It's a rainy morning in Northern Virginia, and the house is quiet. My husband is off to work at the Pentagon, and my children, Ashley and Jacob, are sound asleep. I am embarrassed to tell you that it is 8 a.m., and I just woke up. I planned on starting at 5:30 a.m., but the rain sang a sleepy song and darkness from the clouds kept my room a place for sedation. The Devil was pleased, I am quite sure.

I'm certain I don't have his support in writing this book. I know that in the pages to come there will be a battle. However, after years of battling, I am no longer afraid. Satan should fear us. We should not fear him! I plan on writing not just about my prince and rescuer, but about Satan and how he came to rob and destroy me. However, my rescuer set me free. He also trained me for battle and taught me how to fight *from* victory and not *for* victory.

I was once held captive by fear, generational sin, and other forms of bondage. I was a prisoner bound with chains, but I am free now. I pray that you too will be set free by reading my story. I was so broken, and my brokenness told me that life was not worth living and that God was not God.

Dear reader, as we begin this book together, I should warn you that I will be quite transparent. I believe that the more transparent I am, the more you will see and know the power of the One who saved me. He desires to save you, too! This prince of mine comes to rescue not just me, but all! In fact, my rescuer has a name, Jesus Christ of Nazareth! I pray that if you don't know Him yet, this book will introduce Him to you.

Maybe you doubt that a rescuer exists, or you are angry with Him or question His ways. I get that. In fact, I stopped believing there was a God. I even told Him to go to hell. My hardships in life made me furious with Him and doubt His very existence. I believed He tormented me and was deaf to prayer. I, maybe like you, have thrown my fists at Him and said, "Forget you, God, as you have forgotten me!" I cursed Him! But despite all my fits of rage, He answered me. I will never forget the way He responded—thus this book.

Are you ready to read further? I am asking myself if I am ready to write further. I am nervous! I don't know you, and I am about to share my life with complete transparency. It feels like I am going naked before you. I could easily convince myself never to complete this manuscript. Will you do me a favor? Please be open to this book. It is nonfiction, the true story of a lost person who was found, of a girl searching for a prince in the wilderness. When she did not find Him, He found her.

He waited for me and never gave up! I am doing this for Him as a promise and praise. After all, He did a whole lot for me.

I pray that in some small way I am writing this book for you, too. Friend, sister, and brother, my prayer is for you to know Him and for Him to be your hope and rescuer as He is mine. Looking back over my life, difficult as it was, if my God permitted all of these hardships so that you could be set free and He would be glorified, I have no regret. My trials were worth it.

Not only do I write my story for Him and for you, but for my children and the generations to come. Psalm 78:4 states, "We will not hide these truths from our children; we will tell the next generation about the glorious deeds of the Lord, about His power and His mighty wonders." I want them to know that the Lord Jesus has shown Himself to me with glorious deeds and mighty wonders beyond what any eye could see, any ear could hear, and any mind could fathom (1 Cor. 2:9).

I also want my generations to come to understand that they had a mother, grandmother, and great-grandmother who loved them and warred her best so Satan would not take those future generations. I pray that I will hand them down the same sword that I so actively battled with, the Word of God. May they never forget my story—or how to fight. At the end of the battle, even if they are a bit out of breath, somewhat bruised, and somewhat tired, all that will matter is that they won, thus walking in victory and not defeat. My desire is for them to war for God's kingdom wholeheartedly so that in the end they will hear "Well done, good and faithful servant, well done!"

Dear friend, whether or not we meet on this earth, I want us to meet in heaven. I don't know you, and yet I am compelled to share my life with you. Will you join me now? I am ready to leap by faith.

Love,
Maryann

CHAPTER 1
Waiting for My Prince

I think my bed will comfort me.
And sleep will ease my misery.

—Job 7:13

As a young girl about nine years old, I would go to bed at night believing I was a princess. I would brush my hair before bed and straighten out my covers and pillow to ensure my princess bed did not look messy. My long hair had to lie perfectly over my shoulders, and I would hold my hands tightly together over my chest.

As I closed my eyes, I would worry about being pretty enough for him and wonder, *Will he want to rescue me?* Or, *Will he run when he hears the commotion downstairs?* I knew in my heart I was not princess quality. I was not royalty, and my parents were far from being a king and a queen. Nonetheless, I would dream and await my rescuer. I would lie still all night just waiting, waiting to be awakened by a prince. *Dear prince, please come on time. Don't forget about me!*

As I reflect on my childhood and the fantasy of being rescued by a great prince or knight, I ask myself, *Is that not every little girl's desire, or was it a way for me to escape a dreadful place? Was it "Rescue me, please; I want out of this house," or "Rescue me, I am afraid,"* or *"Rescue me from frightful nights, nights that offer me no comfort as I lie in bed, trembling and afraid?"* I am sure it was a composite of all these things.

The truth is, I wanted a strong and mighty prince who would grant me safety, love, and trust. I wanted a life of peace, love, and joy. Is that too much to ask at age nine? A true prince would hold me when I cried, comfort me in my fear, and promise never to harm or leave me. He would be available. For most of my childhood, I felt alone, afraid, and desperate for safe love. I craved a love that did not hurt, a love that could be trusted. Was this love not found anywhere? Was the prince I so desired as real as Santa Claus? I so badly wanted him to be real.

During those nights when I prepared for my prince's arrival, I would wear my prettiest nightgown, brush my hair, close my eyes, and just wait. *Will he come tonight?* I so hoped to hear and feel him. I knew the touch of his hand and warm embrace would mean my whole life would be changed, and all I had hoped for would come true. I believed he would lean over me and grab my princess hands. He would free me from the harsh walls that surrounded me and say, "Maryann, my little princess, arise. I am here now, and everything is going to be all right. There will be no more tears, no more fears, and I love you. You are beautiful, a delightful sight to see, and your gown is radiant! I am here to take you to that safe place forever." My mind would entertain this thought for the next couple of years.

I especially desired his arrival on the weekends. That's when Dad came home. He liked his alcohol, and we would pay the price for it. Nearly every weekend of my childhood, my dreams of being rescued would be interrupted with screaming, furniture breaking, and police visits. I prayed to God that He would protect us. I heard the name of Jesus in my house every weekend, but it was spoken with slurred speech and horrible breath, and none of us knew Him at all. I just knew His name, and we used that name as a cussword in our home.

On a good weekend, the police did not come, and my mom would not need a new pair of eyeglasses. On a bad weekend, I dressed as a princess before bed only to have the police come into my room and lift up my nightgown to ensure I had no bruises. Sometimes we would go to a shelter for the night. My heart and my mind raced with fear. *Is Mom okay? Is Kriste [my twin] still sleeping? Is she safe? Will the police take Dad from us? Maybe the police will believe me when I tell them he is a good dad when he is not drinking. I can convince them to let him stay!*

As a child and into my teen years, I feared death. Most commonly, I feared my dad would die from drinking and driving or of a heart attack. I also feared Mom being hurt badly. Sometimes in Dad's drunken rage, he would use guns as a threat, and our German shepherd would take a kick or two. I often wondered when my prince would come. *Please come and rescue me from darkness. Dear God, please don't let us be hurt.*

CHAPTER 2
No More Waiting for a Prince!

Cry for help, but will anyone answer you?

—Job 5:1

*I*t was 3 a.m., and I was awakened by a loud crashing noise. *Is Dad home yet? Why is the car horn screaming from the garage?* With my heart racing, I ran for the stairs, following my mother's frustrated, irritated voice only to find that Dad was indeed home. His car was in the garage, but he had driven through the garage to get there. His head was lying on the car horn, which explained the noise. As I watched in horror and shame, my mom lifted his overweight body out of the car and helped him to bed; poor Mom, trying to get Dad up the stairs. His breath created quite a stench, and his seemingly lifeless body made carrying him very difficult for my small-framed mother.

As Kriste and I got older, Mom and Dad moved their room to the basement so we could have our own bedrooms. That also helped Mom, as going down the stairs with a heavy man would be easier. But one night, Mom had had enough of carrying his drunken body, and she dropped him down the basement steps. I will never forget the sound of the fall. I heard crashing glass and a loud thump.

I was having a sleepover that night, and with shame and embarrassment, I ran with my friend down the stairs to see what appeared to be a drunken man at the bottom of the cellar. An entire shelf had been ripped off a wall and lay on top of him. There he was, broken mustard jars and ketchup bottles surrounding his head. During the fall, he apparently grabbed the shelf that held all of our condiments, and everything went down with him. His ear was sliced open, and as I stared at him, I thought, *When, Dad? When is this going to stop?*

My friend was scared by the ordeal. In fact, it was the talk of the school that week. I just wanted to bury my head in the sand. I was humiliated. Soon after that incident, my friend's parents suggested I spend the night at their house instead of mine. Other parents removed me from their children's lives. After all, what parent in his or her right mind would permit a child to associate with such a family? Royalty we were not; we were one of "those" families. I was devastated.

Mom drank, but her behavior was not violent. She would get silly, but she was more reliable and functional when I had a need. I appreciated that. I always felt sorry for Mom. In fact, my heart ached. Dad treated Mom so harshly sometimes. During a heated argument, Mom would often hear "Linda, those are my kids; this is my house, and if you don't like it, get the blank out of here!" Mom knew she had no education and no ability to hold down a job. After all, she never completed the seventh grade. My parents never married, so the house was my dad's property. She was trapped, and she knew it. She was also afraid of Dad and never wanted to fuel his temper.

We all were afraid. When his Lincoln Town Car pulled into the driveway on the weekend, panic would set in because Dad would be so unpredictable. We were not permitted to chew gum, the caps had to be on the shampoo bottles, Kriste had to walk straight (she was pigeon-toed), and Mom had to have the house cleaned, dinner prepared, and bills ready at the table. We never knew what would set him off. We had to be quiet at the dinner table. We were not to speak a word unless spoken to. I was terribly nervous one night during dinner because he was so angry and in such a foul mood. He slammed the salt and pepper shakers, yelled at us, and yelled at Mom. But despite all my anxiety and the complete silence at the dinner table, I got the giggles! I began to squirm in my seat, pretending I was coughing, and before I knew it, I just burst out laughing! And it was no ordinary laugh; I was crying in laughter. The more fear I had about Dad spanking me, the funnier it became! Have you been there?

Well, Dad did not find me at all humorous. He stood up from the table in complete anger, looked at me, and left. I went to my room, where I continued to laugh. It was either to laugh or cry, and I chose to laugh. I was so sick and tired of walking on eggshells and trying to observe random rules that I was going to go insane or make light of the situation.

I never felt sorry for myself, but I always worried about Mom and felt so sorry for my sister. My dad often told her that she was just like her mother. Kriste knew what that meant. It was a way of saying she was dumb, could not do anything right, and was an annoyance. Eventually, his favoritism toward me affected our relationship, and the competition and jealousy would only increase and make Kriste and I war often.

Dad ruled the house with an iron fist. He was permitted to say what he had to say without consequence since we all feared standing up to him. He would receive phone calls and make us leave the house when he was speaking, and when he wanted to watch pornography, Mom would have to take us out for ice cream so he could have the house to himself. I will never forget the stash of pornography I found under his car seat. I must have been nine at the time. I sat in his Lincoln and was shocked at the images I saw. I flipped through each page, never knowing until then what a grown man looked like, but on that day, I become all too familiar with what body parts were used for. *Is that what women are supposed to look like? Is that how women are to act?* Strangely, after seeing his magazines, I went through the house looking for more. I found myself captivated by the images. In fact, when I had the house to myself, I would pop in an R-rated movie and fast forward to the nude scenes. My friends soon realized that their dads had stashes, too, and we would flip through *Playboy* magazines together and laugh and giggle at the very graphic material. I knew more about sex than I wanted to. I must admit that those images brought me to a place where I too wanted to be sexy and provocative looking.

In fact, at age ten or eleven, Dad let us order outfits from the Frederick's of Hollywood catalog. Let's just say that when we went to the bars as a family, we were noticed and it was without good intention. However, Kriste and I enjoyed the attention from these men; it was replacing what was missing in the relationship with our dad. Some of you ladies reading this know what I am talking about. I was a sex image and object and that was all I had going for me. At least that is what I believed. What a lie!

I remember the time Dad called Mom down to the basement, demanding in a loud voice that she please him orally. Of course the term that he used was just as smutty as the magazines he read. She did not want to, and I did not want her to comply with such an order. I felt so sorry that she would be forced to obey. The thought repulsed me! She tried to quiet him down in fear that her daughters might hear. Then she went downstairs and met his request. I was so sickened by the thought of what she was doing that I cried. I had seen enough movies, and I did not want to see my mom that way. No woman should be forced into such an act.

I was determined that day that I would never succumb to such circumstances of abuse in relationships. I was accustomed to this living environment. I eventually adjusted to the lifestyle and assumed my role. I was Dad's favorite, and I had the responsibility of drink maker. My shift started at dark hours in the night. "Maryann! Maryann! Get down here and make your father a drink!" "I'm coming, Dad. Just a minute!" I knew he wanted me to mix whiskey and Coke. I had homework to get through but could not because I was exhausted from these nights.

One evening, he had a friend over, so I got to play bartender for both. After I served them their drinks, his friend looked over at my dad and asked ever so politely, "May I buy your daughter?" As a young girl, I must say I was flattered at such words. *Wow! He thought I was so sweet and pretty that he would want to pay money for me?* In my innocence, I took his request as a great compliment. However, once the kitchen table tipped over and my Dad wrestled his friend to the floor and began to strangle him, I was terribly frightened and screamed for help. Dad told this man that he was going to kill him! The so-called friend was turning blue in the face and apologized profusely. I was confused and did not understand why my dad was so angry. Eventually, I understood clearly.

I was tired and afraid. I was so tired of worrying. I was tired of making drinks, having to protect, be on the lookout, and fear what would come next. If you can't trust your parents, whom can you trust? If you have been down this road, I can feel your pain. If I am opening up past wounds, that is not my intent. However, if you have wounds that need healing, this book will point you to the healer.

On another occasion, we were leaving a restaurant and Dad yet again had too much to drink. I was thirteen and could not drive a vehicle, but since I was Dad's favorite I knew he would listen to me and drive slowly. Dad drove his Corvette to the restaurant, and Mom and the other adults left in another car. I volunteered to go home with my dad because I feared that he would die behind the wheel.

After Dad generously tipped the waitress, we departed. I asked if I could ride home with him, and he slurred yes. My girlfriend went with me so I would not have to be alone. It was a rainy night, and I knew we would have to take Main Avenue to get home. It was a four-lane highway, known for many accidents. When I got in the car, I knew to put a seat belt over my friend and me. Dad was too big for a seat belt, and so I could not get one around him. It was only an eight-minute ride home. *We should be fine,* I told myself. As Dad started the engine, I leaned forward and saw his drunken state; in my fear, I made him promise me that he would not drive fast. He agreed.

As we approached a red light, a car carrying a bunch of teenage boys pulled up beside us. Only my friend and I were visible when they looked into our red Corvette. We were young, but we looked older. The boys decided to rev their engine in hopes that we would race them. I knew things were about to get dangerous. The eight-minute drive home that we had anticipated turned into an hours-long ordeal that included an ambulance, fire trucks, broken glass, a totaled car, and a daughter who could not stop bleeding emotionally for the lack of love or concern that night revealed.

The light turned green, and my drunken dad floored the gas pedal. Yet another promise broken, he launched the car ahead of the boys and then lost control. After spinning several times, we hit a tree. The impact ripped out the car's undercarriage, and only by God's grace did we live. My dad's side was hit, and the entire window exploded on us. Glass was everywhere. My friend and I frantically removed our seat belt and ran out of the car. She was hysterical.

I ran to a house to call the police, and before long, the fire department arrived. The accident scene reeked of booze. There were empty containers in the back seat, and Dad was intoxicated. I almost wished I was, too, so I would stop shaking. The boys who raced us immediately pulled over to make sure we were safe. My dad told them that some punk drivers had run him off the road. "You ran yourself off the road!" the boys said. They realized immediately that Dad was intoxicated and was falsely accusing them of wreckless driving.

I was humiliated, a common feeling for me. I wanted to hide in embarrassment at my father's behavior. Gas oozed from the damaged car; the smell was unmistakable. Just then Dad decided he wanted to smoke. But as he lit his cigarette, three firemen grabbed him to ensure he would not cause an explosion. Witnesses from the restaurant discussed Dad's inebriated state. All of them testified to the guilt of a man who would drink and drive with children. I was hurt more by Dad breaking his promise than I was hurt from the accident. My friend was weeping uncontrollably, traumatized by what had just happened to her, and yet there I was, no tears, no emotion left, numb to the pain I was feeling.

Dad never received one citation for the accident. In Rhode Island, it's not what you know, but who you know. And Dad knew plenty of people, including corrupt people. In fact, Dad was involved in racketeering and organized crime, and I later found out that he and a friend would total cars and make fraudulent claims to insurance companies. The FBI would visit our home later to investigate. My job was to lie and tell them Dad was not home.

I wanted Dad to suffer the consequences for that accident in hopes that maybe a little jail time would make him quit drinking. I secretly wished I had been seriously injured, hoping that a good scare might also make him stop. No such luck, and if that was not enough, he was paid well for totaling the car.

The accident was a reminder that I did not have a dad who would protect me, nor did I have a prince who would save me. Since my prince had failed to come, I gave up on being rescued and started relying on myself. Have you been in a place where you refused to rely on anyone else for fear of being hurt again?

CHAPTER 3

Who Needs a Prince When There Is Jack?

Is not all human life a struggle?

—Job 7:1

*L*et the drinking begin! I may have been twelve years old, but I felt like an adult. So much for childhood and the fantasy of Prince Charming! I had moved on to bigger and better things. *Tonight is the night that I will try Jack Daniels and Coke. My parents do it to cope with misery, and so will I.*

I drank enough that I didn't remember much the next morning. My head hurt, and as I hugged the toilet, praying that the vomiting would stop, I thought, *Is this my future? Will I end up like them? Will I suffer the same afflictions?* But drinking helped me cope with my fear and numbed the pain. I thought, *This is good stuff, and if it works for my parents, it can work for me, too.*

Though I was drinking at age twelve, I managed to hide it from my parents. I was especially careful to hide it from my dad, who was so strict. I learned early on how he felt about drinking and smoking. He would sip his drink from one hand and smoke from the other, all the while telling me I better not do it! I especially knew what he thought of boys. At ten, I was given the speech about how guys would do anything and say anything just to get into my pants. The conversations would always end with a threat: "If you ever get pregnant, I will kill somebody." The fear of having sex worked until he died.

I think Mom knew about my drinking but never really addressed the matter with me. It was as though she understood, as crazy as that may sound. It was her medicine, and she probably assumed I too needed comfort with all the pain in our house. I eventually experimented with marijuana, but alcohol was my medicine of choice.

At thirteen, I realized that I had a drinking problem and that my behavior was becoming a bit risky. When I drank, I had no fear of hurting myself or being hurt.

I vividly remember my best friend and I going to a party with two eighteen-year-olds. We also had plans to see a concert that evening. Of course, the norm was to get your buzz on before going anywhere, and so we did. An entire bottle of wine was most effective. My tolerance at thirteen was pretty high. As we ventured off to the concert, we were on our way to feeling really good. We also smoked some weed that night.

I don't remember too many details about what happened at the concert; I just remember that the band members signed both of my arms with a black Sharpie. I was dressed pretty skimpily, so I was getting a lot of attention from the older crowd, which can be dangerous when you are thirteen. We did not have a ride back from the concert, so we did what I was used to doing: we hitched a ride with an unknown gentleman. He was driving a white Mustang and had a case of beer in the car.

We were quite happy, thinking that the partying had just begun. We had no idea where this man was going to take the three of us, nor did we care. As we headed off to nowhere, we were quickly pulled over by the police because we were white and in a not-so-white part of town. When the officer shined his flashlight into the back of the car and asked our ages, I knew we were busted. I was going to lie, but my best friend answered first, saying she was twelve. Immediately, we were all put in the back of the patrol car, and headed to the police station for trouble.

One of the girls I was partying with pulled a knife on the officer and threatened to kill him. I stayed very quiet. I had no idea that I was partying with a mental case. She was arrested. Finally, the night came to an end once our parents arrived in utter shock to pick us up at 6 a.m.

I feared that my dad would find out. I was his favorite, the perfect one, the smart one who always listened. And here I was drunk, black marker up and down my arms, and looking like a prostitute while sitting in the back of a police car. I begged Mom not to tell him. I feared Dad's wrath. And so he never was informed. However, I have often wondered if finding out might have been a good thing. What if he decided to be more involved and be home more? I will never know.

I have put myself in many dangerous places, and only by God's grace did I remain unharmed. That includes three car accidents involving alcohol, hitchhiking, and blacking out. God must have had a plan in sparing me.

As for the prince I had dreamed of, he never came, and drinking replaced the need for him. It was my rescuer, temporarily getting me through the night with no fear and no pain. Yes, alcohol was my deliverer, especially on the weekends. Like mother, like daughter—I guess the apple does not fall far from the tree. This is a great example of how generational sin gets passed down. I received a bag of bondage from my parents. It included divorce, adultery, pornography, addiction, abuse, and occult practices. I seemed to have little hope of escaping the chains of captivity. And since there was no prince to rescue me, alcohol became my god. It was my master and it controlled me.

CHAPTER 4

Death Knocks

What I always feared has happened to me. What
I dreaded has come true. I have no peace, no
quietness. I have no rest; only troubles to come.

—Job 4:25

I was fifteen years old and playing a great hand of rummy
500 with my dad when I noticed his eyes were yellow. Since
I had just gone out with a great spread and caught him with at
least fifty points in his hand, I thought it would be a good time to
ask a question. "Dad, is it normal for your eyes to be yellow? Your
skin looks a bit yellow, too." Dad finally admitted that he needed
to get checked out.

He had been throwing up bile for a while. He knew he had a
major health problem but ignored the symptoms and continued
drinking. Addiction is powerful. By the time he decided to have an
exam, the alcohol had battered his body to the point of no return.
The doctor's appointment brought a dreaded diagnosis that no
daughter wants to hear and no dad wants to share.

The beginning of my story makes my dad look less than
honorable. There is no doubt that he had a drinking problem and
some dark areas in his life. He could be a very evil man while

under the influence, but Dad without alcohol usually was full of personality, charm, and quick wit.

As stated earlier, my twin and I were a mistake. My parents contemplated having an abortion. But in the end, they made the choice of life for both of us. Thankfully, and regardless of Dad's afflictions, he provided our basic necessities.

Dad worked three jobs to ensure he could provide for his family. He could have walked out on us, but he did not. If financial security equaled an amazing dad, he was pretty amazing in that area. Dad never completed the eighth grade, but taught himself and created a business that was more than enough for us financially. Some of the money, as I would learn later, came from organized crime, but again he provided a roof over our heads. We were not rich, but we definitely had what we wanted when we wanted it. I would have to say that buying for us was Dad's love language. But even with the designer clothes, nice cars, and fine dining, I was left seeking a real relationship with him. He was home on weekends. Since he drank on the weekends, I had just a few hours with him before the battles would begin.

I have asked many questions about my dad's upbringing. I learned that his dad also drank and had a temper. I also learned that he was not treated very well by his dad and was often called the black sheep of the family. Raised in a strict Catholic environment and school, he never really fit in.

Since religion was stuffed down his throat, he never pushed Catholicism on Kriste and me. From what I remember, we attended church twice as a family—once for our infant baptism and the second time for my dad's funeral. I feel as though Dad despised church. Maybe he felt like an outcast. He was not married and had kids, and his reputation and friends were less than reputable.

I will never forget his funeral. The priest who was to deliver the eulogy never showed. If that did not make a girl shake her fist at religion and God, what would? However, his brother ended up taking the role, and I could not have chosen a better person to speak. The eulogy was sentimental and meaningful. But still I will never forget when death knocked.

Waiting for the surgery to be completed, I paced the floors, hoping the doctors could repair my dad's liver. I was not ready to hear the news the surgeon delivered when he walked through those double doors. As I stood there waiting to hear my dad's fate, I begged God that he would be okay. I was angry with my dad for many things, but death was no remedy.

I needed a dad, even if it was just a weekend one. After all, Dad and I had some fun times when he was sober. He would often brag about how beautiful Kriste and I were, and he bragged when I made honors in the eighth grade. He would rip out a card with a picture of the hand soap called Pride and Joy, show it to me, and say, "Maryanneee, you are my pride and joy!" Dad was hilarious! In fact, my sense of humor was learned by him, and I am proud of that. I miss him so much as I write this section of this manuscript. If only he did not drink; if only he were still here.

Dad was a prankster, and most of my friends loved him, though they did not know that other side. There were many things I would not miss about my dad, but there were some things that I was not willing to let go. I cherished many moments with him— the father-and-daughter dances, going to work with him in Connecticut and New Jersey, the times I told his secretaries they had the day off to take me shopping! Dad did not think that was funny, and yet he laughed when we all arrived with bags of clothes!

Christmas and most holidays were days without drinking, and I loved that. With the very little I had, I was so thankful for even those small moments. Strangely, I even have some fond memories of when Dad and Mom were drinking. I remember watching them dance one night while we were at the bar. My job was to put money in the jukebox and play as many Elvis Presley songs as possible. But on this night, "Lady in Red" came on, and Mom and Dad hit the dance floor. When I witnessed that act of love, I began to weep. I was filled with more joy than I could remember because they were getting along while dancing the night away. It was a very short-lived moment, but just the same, it was beautiful to me. Even amid bar smoke and booze, I cherished that moment. I thought, *I hope to have a dance like that someday.*

Little did I know that one day I would dance like that, intoxicated, same bars, same music with the same pain. Our lifestyle was all I knew. To my mind, there was nothing better. I was exposed to darkness, and I was going to make the best out of darkness. And how do you make the best out of darkness? You become dark, too, but I drank in hopes that the darkness would not consume me.

The doctor finally approached us. "I am sorry," he said, "but when we opened up your dad to repair his liver, we found cancer on his pancreas. He has about three months left to live."

My emotions consumed me. I needed a quiet place to process the news. The door with a cross on it led into a dark, private room with a tiny pew and a very small altar, and that became my hiding place. As I sat in that still quiet hospital chapel, I angrily spoke to God. *You, where are you?* I leaned over the pew, crying my heart out. *Why, God? How could you do this? Please don't let him die! I am not ready, God! I am still waiting for him to stop drinking so we can have a family life. I am waiting for him and Mom to reconcile and be happy for once! Why now? I am fifteen! Who will take care of us? I did not get enough time with him sober. Please not now. I will change, God. I will be good. I will stop drinking, too.*

Bargaining always tends to be a last resort, and so there I was at fifteen bargaining with God in hopes that He would permit my dad to live. Bargaining proved to be successful, as Dad lived another year and a half, which was unheard of.

I gratefully had a sober dad during that time, since he had to quit drinking. I watched him face terminal illness with great strength and bravery. Dying, he could still laugh and pull pranks. He would often say, "Only the good die young." He had a huge scar on his stomach from the incisions made during surgery. The scar was shaped like a *T*, and so he would say that he had his initials carved on his stomach.

Sadly, during that last year and a half with Dad, my drinking increased and my desire to be home decreased. With Dad in and out of the hospital, and my selfish desires to live life, I became resentful of having to visit only to watch him gradually perish. The smell of hospitals repulses me. They smell of death. I had to escape that dark place, and so I did by avoiding it.

I knew Dad was nearing the end of his life when he granted my mother all authority in making decisions over us. On that particular occasion, I had asked Dad if I could spend the night at a friend's, and his response pierced my heart. "Go ask your mother," he said. "It is up to her now." I left in tears that night, knowing he was giving up the battle and it would not be long before I was fatherless. *Why God? Why?*

To make matters worse and the pain more intense, I never said goodbye. Our last day together took me by surprise. I never really accepted that he would leave me. I was familiar with the emergency hospital visits. We were in and out of the hospital, and that was our routine. Dad always came home. But this morning would be our last.

When an ambulance responded to Dad's 911 call, I assumed I would meet him later at the hospital as I always did. When they carried my dad up the basement stairs from his bedroom, our eyes met, and his gaze was distant. I just went about my business, getting ready to see him later. Mom went with Dad in the ambulance, and before I knew it, she was home in my bedroom, telling me, "He is gone, Maryann. He is gone." Mom sobbed, and in disbelief I searched the house for Kriste. She immediately drove to the hospital to see his lifeless body one last time.

I did not have the courage to do so, and even today I greatly regret not having one last hug, one last kiss, and one last "I love you, Dad." He was forty-six when he died, and now that I am thirty-four, I consider that to be young.

The hardest and bravest thing I witnessed my dad do was sit us down and tell us he was dying. As a mom, I could not imagine having to share such news with my children. In the fifteen years of my life, I had never seen my dad cry, but on that day, he sobbed. We all did.

Our last Christmas together was a memorable one. We sat on the couch together and listened to the song Dad wanted us to remember him by, Whitney Houston's "And I Will Always Love You." I can hear it now in my head and picture that Christmas. I can see us there on that couch, crying. In fact, I am crying again. I miss him! You may wonder if I forgave him for the rough times. Of course I have. I have chosen to be grateful for what I had and to sympathize with him, since he was obviously a hurting man.

I took my children to his grave two years ago, and in that moment I told him that I was so sorry for the life he had. He masked a lot of pain with drinking. How can I judge him when I have done the same?

My biggest wound is that I know what he is missing and I wish he were here for me. I wondered what it would be like to share the gospel with him. Would we pray together? Could I have led him to Christ? Would he be proud of me? What would he think of Ashley and Jacob or my husband? Furthermore, what would he think about me serving in the military and completing graduate school? Would he say what I so longed to hear again, "I am so proud of you for the woman you have become?" I loved my dad, and I never doubted that he was proud of me. I just desperately wanted to hear those words again. And the coldness of his grave was a reminder of the great loss I had felt. Addiction robbed our family of so much, and sadly addiction was beginning to rob me, too, by the time Dad died.

Dear Reader, I have included many details about my dad, things I am not proud of, but I did not write such things for you to judge him. I wrote them in hopes that part of my story would speak to you. We have no room to judge anyone, lest we be hypocrites. You are reading about a broken man with a broken family, but that brokenness was part of the plan. My dad is part of my story, and his ways made me seek a rescuer. Would I have sought to be saved in a healthy environment? Praise God for brokenness! You will understand what I mean as you read further.

I experienced things that a child should not have to experience. As a mom of two children, I have visualized my babies experiencing just one of the nights I endured as a child, and the rage within could almost devour me. My anxiety is equivalent to the fear I would feel if I left them among ravenous wolves. No child should have to experience such living conditions. However, this book is not meant to condemn my parents in any way. I risk being transparent in hopes of bringing glory to my rescuer. The more you know about my life, the more He will be glorified. You may be wondering at this point about my dad's salvation. I am not sure about his salvation. That hurts. But I do know that I serve a just and merciful God.

CHAPTER 5
Mom's Breakdown

He will not let me catch my breath,
but fills me with bitter sorrows.

—Job 9:18

It was roughly midnight, and instead of sleeping over at a friend's house, I decided to check in with Mom. As I pulled up, I realized there was another vehicle in the driveway, a truck that I did not recognize. Who could be here? Was it a friend helping her cope? It had been only three months since we buried my dad, so having company was still normal. But on this night, it was a bit late to have company. I was about to meet a woman who looked like my mother but was no longer acting like her.

I walked up the front steps and found that the door was locked. Mom never locked us out of the house. I banged on the door and rang the doorbell; she finally appeared. When she opened the front door, she was hesitant about letting me in. "What are you doing here?" she asked. "Mom, I live here," I answered. She did not want to let me in and asked that I sleep somewhere else. After a mild shove, I entered.

Immediately I saw the blankets from my bed on the living room floor next to the fireplace. I saw a body under the covers and was repulsed to see a man I didn't know sleeping in my house, under my covers. As I stormed in, I noticed a joint on the table and beer cans everywhere. Mom always kept the house spotless, so the mess was not normal for her. I had enough beer in me to make me brave, so I decided to take it upon myself to ask the man to leave. I flipped my lid. I cussed him out and told him, "My dad is not even cold in his grave yet. Get out!" But once I realized I was outnumbered, I left, never to sleep another night in that house.

Randomly, I would check in at home. Each time, the house looked worse and worse. Mom started writing "F-you" on the walls and breaking the cabinets. One day, as I sat on the couch in hopes of having a discussion with Mom about what was going on, her boyfriend plopped down next to me and had the audacity to touch a strand of my hair and twirl it between his fingers. He looked at me and said, "You are a beautiful girl. Do you know that?" As I held down my emotions and disgust, Mom walked in, and as she sat down, I stood up and excused myself. What she said next pierced my soul. She sat down and looked up at me and then preceded to tell me that I killed my father. There was a sting in her voice that left me confused and wounded. I later learned that she was bipolar and schizophrenic. And her mental illness was just the beginning of a nightmare I could not awake from.

Slowly things like the big-screen TV and air conditioners went missing. My dad's jewelry mysteriously disappeared. I realized that the man Mom had been sleeping with was robbing us blind. My hate and anger toward people and God boiled! Oh, how I questioned and criticized God for my living hell. *How much harder could things get, God? Will you take anything else from me?*

As things began to vanish, I instantly thought about my dad's 49ers jacket. This guy had the audacity not only to move in on my life, but to wear my dad's clothes and jewelry and wear my mother! *Sorry to be so blunt! Is this a living hell that I am in? Where are you God! You can go to hell for letting this happen! Why don't you find someone else to pick on! I have enough turmoil to last the rest of my life God!*

Nearly every Sunday I would watch the football games with Dad. He would call his bookie before each game, and I was his good luck charm. I loved that! When he won, we celebrated and I went on a shopping spree, but when we lost, Dad would drink a bottle of Pepto and lose thousands. Sometimes we would bear the brunt of his anger. Nonetheless, I wanted that jacket. I searched high and low and failed to find it. It was gone!

My extensive search through the entire house left me frustrated, enraged and out of breath with my heart racing. *Where is it? Not my dad's jacket, too!* I realized that Mom's man of the hour must have the jacket. I could handle losing all the other things this man had helped himself to, including my mom, but my dad's jacket was out of the question! In fact, Dad's best friend had asked for that jacket, and I was so pleased eventually to give it to him. I will never forget the day of my dad's funeral and the sound of his friend's weeping.

I knew exactly the bar where I could find Mom and her boyfriend, and after downing a bottle of wine, a friend and I drove there. I was the only sixteen-year-old in that skanky place. The crowd froze when I walked in because I clearly did not belong there. I asked for Mom's boyfriend by name, and someone pointed me in his direction. There he was, sitting at the bar with Mom, and behold, he was wearing my dad's jacket.

Never in my life had I felt such rage. My body and my voice were trembling. Tears formed and began to run down my face. My rage sustained me. I marched right over to that man with a boldness that even the wine could not offer. I slapped him so hard in the face that you could hear the sound the moment my hand met his cheek. The impact felt incredible. It was as though a weight had been lifted off my chest. I had been so tired of losing, that this one night of winning was a great victory.

The bar fell to a complete silence, all eyes on me, all eyes on him. I loudly demanded my deceased father's jacket. I got it, turned around, and never looked back. I heard my mom lean over to him and say, "I am sorry she did that, but you are wearing her daddy's jacket." I wanted to say, "Thanks for the consideration now, Mom. I could have used it a few weeks ago when I saw the man wrapped in my comforter in front of the fireplace where we sang and said our goodbyes to Dad!"

I had no intention or desire of ever seeing my mother again. She was a whore in my book, and a drunk bar queen, one that trader her daughters for men and booze. How my hate for her would eventually change, but I never imagined I would have to wait a painful fourteen years to see her again and in those years of waiting fear her dead.

CHAPTER 6
Losing Our Home

Let the day of my birth be erased
and the night I was conceived.

—Job 3:3

ad taught me before he died how to handle the bills. When I was fifteen, he sat me down and explained how to write out checks and balance the checkbook. He could not trust my mom to pay the bills because she was unable to grasp such things. I was told that the taxes on the house would be deferred until the house was sold. I paid the bills as best I could. We received Social Security after my father's death, but soon that money would be squandered on my mom's new lifestyle and new man. We barely had food.

Arriving home one night, I was hungry and noticed Mom had cooked a meal on the stove. As I reached for it, she told me it was off limits because it was for her man. There was no toilet paper in the house, and food was limited. The house was being destroyed and so was my soul. I became so angry with life. I began drinking during the week and that became my crutch. But I still had a house to take care of, or at least I thought I did.

The city sent a letter saying we owed back taxes on the house. I drove down to city hall to explain that we were tax deferred until the house was sold. I sat in the parking lot, wondering why I had so much responsibility when all my friends were granted the privilege of studying for SATs and shopping for prom dresses. And there I was, trying to run the show for survival. I sat there feeling bitterness and resentment over the death of my dad and the loss of my mom to alcohol, mental illness, and men. I felt so alone, unloved and not worth love. Otherwise my dad would have picked me over booze and mom would pick me over men. I was so convinced that no one cared and that I was just a mistake. I concluded that men were not princes and that there was no God. I eventually stopped seeking Him and praying to Him for help. As far as I was concerned, the world was godless, and so were the people.

The city hall clerk's look told me she did not want to deal with a sixteen-year-old kid who lacked the capacity to understand that the city needed money and wanted it now. We owed about $5,000 in back taxes, and I was told that unless I paid the money, our house would be auctioned off. Not a good day for me. And shortly after my visit to City Hall, the house was sold for less than half of its value. We took an incredible loss, but who would want a house that looked like a bunch of bandits and graffiti gurus lived there?

For a moment I thought, *There goes my entire life!* My dad, my mom, and now the very house I was raised in were gone. *What's next?* I would ask myself. How could it get any worse? At sixteen, I was homeless, parentless, and hopeless. Oh wait, maybe I should pray to a silent God that ignores… I won't waste my time.

As for my remaining high school years, they were a joke. I would get Fs on all my tests and think sarcastically, *Really? I failed another trig test, duh!* The teachers would say, "Maryann is absent more than she is present." How correct they were! What they failed to realize is that even on those days when my body was present, my mind was still absent.

The guidance counselor was the only one who knew about my situation. My uncle had notified her of my dad's death. Looking back, I realize she was so good to me. I never spoke a word to her about anything, and yet she showed compassion toward me and believed in me. She would talk to me about college and college prep classes. I would always agree with her suggestions mostly because I liked her. I graduated from high school, though by no means with honors. I was drunk most of my high school days, and to have graduated with no accountability to anyone is truly amazing.

But what college would want my GPA? With all my failures, in my emotional state, and with my addiction, what college would accept me? Statistically, the odds were against me. The world would look at me as a young lady with a grim future. Maybe a teen pregnancy, drug overdose or multiple children with different fathers would be the climax of my future? Or I would marry a man just like my dad and be abused and booze would hold me in the midnight sorrows?

But the world and the Word are very different. The world says, "No future, worthless, failure, with little chance of making it." But the Word of God is quite contrary to the world. The Word said I had hope and a future. I am living proof that the Word is truth.

I would eventually wind up at the last school I could ever have imagined myself attending, a very conservative Christian school named Liberty University. I chuckle even writing the name! The old me would never have desired a school like that, nor would I have paid for such strict discipline and boredom! *What is wrong with coed drinking? Put your Bibles down, people, and have some fun!* Fresh out of high school, I would not have made it past the first interview! Oh, and did I mention the dress code? Short skirts and bling was my thing!

CHAPTER 7

Painful Relationships

The Lord examines both the righteous and the
wicked. He hates everyone who loves violence.

—Ps. 11:5

I am sure you are wondering whether I dated or had sex with
boys. Who wouldn't assume that based on my lifestyle?
Surprisingly, because my dad was so strict, I was afraid to have sex,
and I thank him for that. I was in a relationship and my boyfriend
eventually asked for my hand in marriage. I was only seventeen,
and the day after my senior prom, we were married. Mom signed
the papers, and off I went two thousand miles away from home
for the next four years of my life. Marriage was an easy "out" for
a girl that needed a home and food on the table. I also needed to
be loved, and marriage seemed to bring forth a comfort in time
of great loss and abandonment.

The marriage relationship was not healthy and abusive, but
looking back, I praise God for all the trials. They helped me to see
what my childhood wounds were doing to me and to realize that
my life was destructive. I did not know how to be a wife or how to
handle my rage. I would run in the face of conflict and retaliate
at the highest level when I was hurt. I was suspicious, mistrustful,
and always waiting for something bad to happen.

My first husband and I were a recipe for disaster the moment we said our vows. I was a raging, wounded girl who was not going to let another person hurt her. When you are a young girl raised in a dysfunctional environment, you tend to think it is normal, but when divorce becomes reality, it is evident that you are a broken person in need of repair.

After my divorce, I became numb from my brokenness and found myself in and out of relationships. I attracted men who were much like my dad, and I became involved in a series of abusive relationships.

For a child reared in such an environment, abuse sometimes means love, and you believe that somehow you can change the abuser. But from what I have learned along my destructive path, we don't change people, God does. So if you are trying to change a spouse, a man, or woman in your life, stop trying to play God, release yourself from that burden, and completely let go of any abusive relationship. If you are married to an abuser, seek safety first and then arrange godly counseling from a pastor or professional. Cling to God and be freed from your prison walls!

My mind was so warped from my upbringing that I thought a man bent on controlling me must love me. But if a man bruises you, slaps, bites, or pinches, calls you a whore, or uses any other language that degrades you, you are setting yourself up for complete destruction if you stay with him. I have experienced these things. If a man controls you, he is your master and you are his slave. The Word says that whatever controls you, that is your master and you are a slave to that master (Rom 6:16). This is true not just in an abusive situation, but with drugs, alcohol, pornography, or whatever else may ensnare you. You decide who your master will be. I pray you will choose God and be free.

My abusive relationships with men left me utterly empty and my spiritual condition in complete ruins. But I have been restored because I am now in relationship with the right man, Jesus. Jesus is a man who will never forsake you, never harm you, and never make you tremble in fear. He brings forth peace and loves like no other! He heals our wounds! He is a man who will treasure you and die for you. If you are in a place of despair like I was, I want you to know that you are worth so much more. If you are reading this and feel there is no way out, you are buying into a lie. That is a lie from the Devil. You can be restored. I am completely restored, and may the rest of these chapters be evidence of who the restorer is. And may the next victory story be yours! What are you waiting for?

CHAPTER 8
Rock Bottom

My spirit is crushed and my life is nearly
snuffed out. The grave is ready to receive me.

—Job 17:1

The pain from my past controlled me, and the pain of my dysfunctional life was consuming me. I remember so clearly the day when I was going to take a bottle of pills. After getting slapped around in the car, I arrived home. I ran down the stairs, praying for the courage to end my life. My body was trembling, my mind was racing, and my heart was palpitating. I fled into the bathroom, hoping to escape him. I opened the mirror door to find a full bottle of Tylenol.

As I slammed the bathroom door shut, I realized my dog, my faithful friend, was in there with me. He was all I had to go home to. My sweet dog had also suffered from the abusive environment. He was picked up and thrown one time because he intervened on my behalf. As I popped open the pills, they flew everywhere because I could not contain my trembling. I was in terrible emotional pain, and I wanted it to end.

As my angry pursuer beat down the door, I first tried to pick up the pills and then jumped into the bathtub and lay there as far away from the door as I could get, knowing that in just a few seconds, I was going to get it again. I remember hearing my body hit the sides of the tub from all my trembling. My poor dog jumped in and sat on top of me, barking at the loudness of pounding fists against the bathroom door. I screamed, "Stop it! Just stop it!" The tears rolled off my cheeks. *I'm so sick of this life. When will this stop? I need to drink something to make this panic stop!*

My mother's words came naturally from my mouth. "Stop it! Get out of the girls' bedrooms!" Stop it! Leave me alone! One night my cousin intervened when Dad was trying to choke my mom, and his entire arm went through a glass window. I will never forget that sight—the glass, the blood, the screaming. And there I was, following in her footsteps. What a dreadful future that awaited me. *Where are you, God? Are you going to help me? Where is my prince?*

After yet another night of drinking and fighting, I was desperate for help. Blacking out was becoming the norm for me. Out of desperation, I ran to a friend's house for comfort. I could confide in her. She would take me in and be my drinking companion.

She offered me a place to stay, and I considered it. She convinced me that I needed to flee from this relationship. She told me that she and her husband would help me. But after a night of drinking, little did I know that they were luring me to participate in acts that I clearly would not willingly condone. Despite repeatedly saying no, I awoke the next morning to the reality that a nightmare had taken place. I had blacked out that night, and that morning my self-worth shriveled. I was now damaged goods.

I condemned myself and I hated myself for what had happened. I was so angry about what they did and disgusted with myself for letting alcohol rob me of my ability to protect myself. A mere "Sorry, Maryann, we let things go too far" was not going to shake the pain or diminish the violation and betrayal. The shame and blame consumed me, and it would be years before I would share this incident. I was shattered and tormented with humiliation. Without family, to whom do you run? My friends were not trustworthy considering that I was used and abused by the very person who was going to help me!

To cope with my latest wounds, I drank more. But in sober moments, I had to face the wreckage I was becoming. After running to alcohol most of my life, one day my despair consumed me. Alcohol was no longer helping me. I was afraid of my suicidal thoughts, and these thoughts made me run to God. Thoughts of ending your life are a sign of desperation, as is showing up for work still under the influence. In complete despair and need of help, I decided to try God one more time.

I was at work at a portrait studio and still intoxicated from the night before. I thought, *If there is a God, He surely would not want anything to do with me.* And I was so angry that I did not want Him, either. But the floodgates were about to be opened because the pain was too heavy to bear, and out of complete despair and desperation, I took my chances on running to God regardless of my assumed reputation with Him and my anger toward Him. If there was a God, He was all I had left, but the question remained, would He still be willing to talk to me?

My life was toxic, and I was quite sure I was a terrible stench in God's nostrils. I knew my breath that morning was awful; I smelled like a brewery. I was still feeling a buzz and was not yet sober. I wanted out of life; I wanted to check out permanently. Have you ever been there?

Filled with fear and despair, I went into a back office. It was the size of a closet. There was just enough space for props that were used for portraits, old portraits, a table, and a mirror. As I turned to close the office door for privacy and a safe place to unleash my pent-up emotions, I asked myself, *Why are you doing this,*

Maryann? Why now? And what if He does not answer you? Then what? God is not real, and yet you are about to get on your knees to empty space. However, there was a yearning and another voice in my head that said, *You have nothing else left but to call out just one more time in hopes that maybe this time God will respond.*

I struggled to keep doubt and fear from invading my mind, and fell to my knees before this empty space. The weight from my wounded past and present felt as though it would crush me. And while I was on my knees, the weight of my losses pressed in on me.

With warm tears streaming, I cried out, "God, help me. Don't forsake me now! I am desperate for you. I don't know if you are real, I don't know if you care, but please, oh please, don't leave me this way! God, I don't want to live, and I am afraid to die. I am weary of waking up to the weight and pain of life. But I am scared because if there is no God, I have nowhere left to run but to my very own grave. Show me you love me and that you hear me! I don't want to be alone anymore and afraid. I need to know you are real, please show me a sign that I will be alright."

Then in silence I wept. I began to weep for my mom, weep for my sister, weep for my father, weep over his death, weep from my brokenness, and weep in my hopes for more. I gave it all to God on my knees in that moment; I don't even know what I said. I could barely breathe. I just know that I wept so much that I thought I was losing my mind. Then, slowly getting up from my knees, I looked in the mirror to see a girl who was broken and exhausted from carrying the load of life on her own. Mascara ran down my cheeks. I said to myself, *See. No answer, no God, and I will never get on my knees again!* Well, some of us tend to speak too soon.

CHAPTER 9
A Little Old Man

And call upon me in the day of trouble; I
will deliver you, and you will honor me.

—Ps. 50:15

As I walked out of the back office, I looked at my schedule. It was a quiet day, no appointments scheduled, which was nice. I did not want to put on the facade of happiness and contentment when in reality I wanted to check out. Ironically, here I was taking pictures and managing a portrait studio built on capturing the images of smiling families and children. I saw in those photos what I longed for: family, security, and love.

Within minutes of walking out of the office, I had an encounter divinely orchestrated by the One to whom I had just spoken.

As I stood at the portrait studio counter, a little old man approached. He had on a yellow baseball cap. "Sir, may I help you?" I asked. He said nothing. I asked again as his gaze pierced right through me. I thought he may have noticed I had been crying, and I felt uncomfortable. I asked yet again, "Sir, may I help you?" No answer.

At this point, I realized that he could not hear or speak. He began to smile at me warmly, and I smiled back. He then slipped a card to me and tapped on it three times. I thought he was handing me a note detailing what he needed in his portrait.

That was not the case. In complete disbelief, I read, "Angel of God, my Guardian Dear, for whom His love permits us here, ever this day be at my side to light, guard, rule, and guide." The flip side of the card carried a picture of a large angel watching two children cross over a broken bridge. In my mind, the children were my twin and I. Tears welled in my eyes, and as the tears ran down my face, each one fell on that card. When I read it, I knew that God had heard me, and I was utterly stunned beyond belief.

I looked up from the card and that precious little old man in a yellow cap was gone! I never saw him again. I paced the store, hoping I could ask how he knew. But he was gone! "See, I am sending an angel before you, to guard you on the way and bring you to the place I have prepared" (Ex. 23:20). I am crying at this moment yet again because I will never forget that day. It was the beginning of change. From that day forward, I knew that I was loved by God, and that brought me an incredible and unshakable security. I was loved! *God loves me! I am going to be okay.*

After looking for the little old man, I returned to that small office, and this time, there was no haunting voice telling me God was not real. No! I heard a voice that said, "I am real, Maryann, and I have always loved you!"

I dropped to my knees, and all I could utter amid my sobs was, "Thank you. Thank you for hearing my prayer. Help me, God, to change my ways and my life. I can't do this alone. Thank you for giving me hope." And before I knew it, I was not in fear, I was in peace. I believe that was the first time I had ever spoken those words to God. I meant them with all my heart, and today I have said those words more times than I can count because I love Him!

I can't explain to you the courage that came over me that day. There was boldness, and that empty space in the office became a sacred place. There is a God, and he heals the brokenhearted and binds up their wounds (Ps. 147:3). I wish I could tell you that I was saved in that office, but the pages to come will prove that I was not yet set free. That experience revealed a God, but I did not yet know about His Son. I was still lost, but being lost after an encounter with God means there is hope for yet another. As God would have it, I was about to know Him not just by name, but by consuming love that would transform me for the rest of my life!

CHAPTER 10
A Failed Attempt at New Beginnings

My eyes are swollen from weeping and I
am but a shadow of my former self.

—Job 17:7

The marriage ended, and I moved in with my sister in Pennsylvania. Three half-siblings from Mom's first marriage were living there. Mom had moved to Florida where her dad tended to her mental illness, but her drinking continued.

Living with my family after four years of living two thousand miles from home felt like the right thing to do. My twin sister and I became great drinking buddies. Since we shared life together from the womb, we did everything together. And partying is what we knew best. She and I would drink and reminisce about our childhood. We would often talk about Dad's fits of rage and hot temper.

Dad harshly mistreated my poor sister. We were both wounded from our childhood, but her wounds seemed to be much deeper than mine. As Dad's favorite, I had the job of holding down the fort, providing an ear for Dad to vent, and making him mixed drinks, but Kriste often heard that she was just like Mom and that was no compliment. She got the belt more often than I did. She was disciplined heavily for wetting her bed and for walking pigeon-toed. Kriste needed bars on her feet to correct them, and if she did not walk right, she would learn quickly not to forget the next time, since she would be reprimanded publicly, sometimes in front of Dad's drinking pals. I can see her now being spanked and put in a corner at a cookout for not walking correctly. Kriste would often receive bad grades in school, which I believe was a result of our environment. I believe she had major anxiety, and who could learn under such conditions? Dad would push her. He would make her memorize cards and then quiz her. If she failed in any way, she was penalized.

So Kriste and I would talk about the devastation in our lives. We would talk about hiding under the kitchen table crying while waiting for the police to come and about the shelter we were forced to live in. Drinking together was not the healthiest outlet for the pain, but it seemed to work for the moment.

My life was becoming yet another train wreck waiting to happen. Since my divorce, the drinking had increased, which I did not think was possible. But worse than that, so did the relationships with men. Can you say "more pain?" I seemed to attract controlling and abusive men. It was as though they sensed my vulnerabilities. But, even in the midst of all the drinking and chaotic living, my emptiness and grief often made me reflect on the moment in the portrait studio. Would I ever have another encounter like that? Was God angry at me?

One evening, my sister and I went to a house party. We had planned on spending the night, since I did not want to drink and drive. I went to bed earlier than everyone else because I had to work the next morning. I was drunk, and I needed to sleep it off before morning.

That night, sleeping in a stranger's house, I awoke with the sense that evil was surrounding me. My heart was racing, and I felt as though something terrible was in the room with me. I awoke at about 3 a.m. with the hair standing up on my neck, and I felt the sensation of something sitting on my chest. I instantly asked God to protect me, and as I lay there in total darkness and fear, I saw a man standing to the right of my bed. He was robed in white, but I could not see his face because I was paralyzed with fear and could not move. I heard the man say in a quiet voice, "Say, 'I believe, I believe, I believe!'" I did as he asked. Instantly, the darkness left and I went back to sleep.

The next morning I kept replaying in my mind what had happened. What was that encounter about? As a Catholic, I knew of Jesus, and I wondered if He was the man standing on the right side of my bed, intervening on my behalf against some kind of darkness that sought me that night.

CHAPTER 11
Joining the Military

O God, you know how foolish I am; my
sins cannot be hidden from you.

—Ps. 69:5

I was now twenty-one and decided to join the Air Force.
I was tired of working as a portrait studio manager and
wanted to make something out of my life. I wanted to attend
college, too. My last attempt to attend college had been a disaster.
A man with whom I was in relationship had ripped my textbooks
to pieces, so I quit college and had decided never to go back.

However, I really wanted to get my degree. I also desired a
new beginning as a way to escape. I knew I did not want to be like
my mother. She was uneducated and lacked the ability to sustain
herself on her own. She was told all throughout my childhood that
the house was not hers, and if she did not like her living conditions,
there was the door. Mom was so dependent and fragile. I was
going to be a strong woman, educated, and would never depend on
a man! *Ever!* Depending on a man meant shelters, abuse, control,
forced sex, living in and out of project housing, and going through
shelter boxes for next year's school clothes. No man was going to
hurt me again, and no man would ever tell me what to do. I had
had enough. I would hurt them before they hurt me!

So I enlisted in the air force in January 1998. I was sent to Columbus Air Force Base in Mississippi after completing basic training and technical school. I became a life support technician and would spend the next four years working with fighter pilots. The military is not exactly the best place for a newly divorced twenty-one-year-old with a drinking problem. Drinking is highly encouraged among the military community, and I fit right in. Disaster was just waiting to happen. As a woman in the military, you have quite a group to select from when it comes to dating, and select I did. But between the drinking and relationships nothing could fill the void. I was seeking love and acceptance but instead received more pain from the choices I made. I tended to attract men who were just like my dad. They were controlling and abusive. These relationships confirmed that I should not trust any man. Years ago, Mom told me, "They are all the same, Maryann," and I believed it. After all, she knew that firsthand.

My drinking nearly cost me my career after I was pulled into the commander's office yet again for drinking in the officers club and mingling too closely with the pilots. My commander's main concern was fraternization. Enlisted airman are to keep "professional only" relationships with all officers. I neglected to do so weekly. They bought me drinks, and that's all that mattered. The officers did not seem a bit concerned, and so unprofessional relationships became the norm.

One night I ended up in the emergency room after partying all night with the wrong crowd. I was convinced that someone had slipped something into my drink when I had severe heart palpitations and my body was tingly all over. I feared being given a random drug test because a failed drug test meant a dishonorable discharge from the military, and I did not want to lose my career. But, even with that scare, there I was again back at the same bar with the same crowd.

Alcohol had such a stronghold on me. I no longer had control over alcohol; it controlled me. I put myself in many dangerous places, and realized that I had a big problem. I lacked any regard for my life, and I was slowly deteriorating from the inside out. I found myself in more bad relationships, with more pain and more drinking. I was stuck on a merry-go-round and wanted off! I just could not heal from the losses in my past, and gripped by fear, I was always waiting for something terrible to happen. I was always expecting the worst and dreading the next.

My fears were confirmed yet again when I received a call from an air force doctor who told me that pre-cancerous cells were found in an exam and that I needed immediate medical attention. I was stunned to the core. Secretly, I had always feared cancer after my father's diagnosis. I still battle that fear every now and then. The diagnosis and the two surgeries I endured made me fear dying, and I decided to seek God again. I knew my lifestyle was not a healthy one, but at the age of twenty-two, I never imagined fearing a terminal diagnosis. Both of my grandmothers had died of cancer as well, so I was a high-risk patient.

Fearing the loss of my health, I started thinking about dying. I wondered where I would go if I died. Did the God who met me in the portrait studio remember me still, or had He turned away in disgust because of my sinful lifestyle? I was about to find out.

CHAPTER 12
Seeking God

If my people, who are called by my name,
will humble themselves and pray and seek
my face and turn from their wicked ways,
then will I hear from heaven and will
forgive their sin and will heal their land.

—2 Chron. 7:14

*A*fter the health scare, I decided to reevaluate my life. In doing so, I realized that I was empty. Even though I had the Air Force, financial security, a fun job, was in a relationship, attended college, worked out (and had great abs), I was a mess on the inside! I am sure the world looked at me and assumed I had a wonderful life, but I was falling apart, nothing filled the dark hole in my soul. The more I acquired the more disappointed I became because the next "big thrill" did not fix me. Have you ever felt that way?

I decided to hit the mountains for a mountain bike excursion. I had always loved the outdoors. I felt God in His creation. I wanted to get my head straight. I also thought I would begin seeking the God who met me in the portrait studio. I went with a boyfriend and unfortunately was too distracted to make time for what I had planned. The biking and scenery as well as the crowd of friends did not leave room for a "sacred place." Besides, I did not want them to know I was seeking God. I did not want them to think I was a freak! I came to realize however, that even though I decided to not seek God, he began to seek me.

As God would have it, we stopped for a lunch break during our road trip to the mountains, and one of the guys in our group took time to pray over his food. You may be a Christian and think, *Well what is the big deal?* Understand, that in my household, even though we called ourselves Catholic, we never prayed over our meals unless it was Christmas or Thanksgiving! Remember, I had been to church only twice with my family. This gal was shocked! In fact, I was a bit uncomfortable with him bowing and praying, as were the rest of the guys in our group. However, from that point forward, I had my eye on this "holy roller." I studied him the entire trip because deep down I did not think his prayer was a coincidence—I went on a trip, planning to seek God, and I saw this guy pray over his food!

All of us in the group drank, but he didn't; we used foul language, but he didn't. We were not a humble crowd by any means—all the guys in my group were fighter pilots—but he was humble. If you have yet to meet a fighter pilot, you will have no doubt when you do because he will tell you! Not all pilots were this way, but most were. That was the interesting thing about this praying guy: he was truly humble. He never spoke about himself; he just listened as though he had nothing to prove. He stood out from the rest, unlike me, always blending in with the world.

I got a chance to share a few laughs with the religious guy. Actually, I made fun of him for wearing Blistex because it looked like it went everywhere but on his lips! I never asked him about his faith, and I am glad he did not ask about mine! The trip ended, and I never did have my "God moment." Or did I?

CHAPTER 13

Who Is This God?

Always be prepared to give an answer
to everyone who asks you to give the
reason for the hope that you have.

—1 Peter 3:15

*W*eeks went by after that mountain bike trip, and the relationship I was in ended. I wasn't surprised, since my drinking tended to scare people away, as did my character. I was not a healthy girlfriend; I had too much baggage, to say the least.

I never expected much in relationships, which isn't surprising because I had only my parents' example. I wanted to hurt men before they could hurt me. I always felt like I was in a competition with them. I had to be better. I seemed so confident and secure on the outside, but on the inside I heard *You are not good enough. You never will be.*

I would date for a while, meet the man's family, and immediately become ashamed of mine. I would think, *if they only knew.* That other family seemed so healthy, so perfect, and so complete. I did not have that luxury and was incredibly insecure because of it. Plus I was divorced! What momma would want her son with a divorced chick? Worse yet, an orphaned drunk? Admit it. Reading my story thus far, you would not want little Johnny in a relationship with

47

me! Shoot, I have a son now, and I would tell him to run! If you were a Christian mom, I was a bad girl going to hell! And my goal was to hurt little Johnny before he hurt me!

As a life support technician in a fighter squadron, you work with fighter pilots basically 24/7. In fact, I acted like a fighter pilot without a jet. I was just as morally sound as they were—not a compliment here. I loved my job, and I cared a great deal for some of the people I worked with, but I also had my problems.

Sexual harassment is a large issue in the military, and zero tolerance is not a reality. My first encounter with this problem came during technical schooling in Texas. I was at an enlisted bar and in uniform, since I had not completed enough phases to be permitted to wear civilian clothes. As a new airman, I had not achieved enough rank yet, so I was at the bottom of the totem pole. In uniform, there are many rules to follow. You must salute officers, wear your hat appropriately, and remain in regulation at all times. I did all that on this particular night, but I was still bait the moment I walked into this club.

I had spent two hours mingling with classmates when up came a staff sergeant who had had way too many drinks even to shout commands. However, with all the slurred profanity he directed toward me, I became the center of attention. The sergeant told a friend, "Watch what I do to this girl." He said, "Airman, over here now!" I reported directly to this very angry man. He said, "You f-ing stand here until I am through with you." I have to admit I was afraid. As a group of enlisted people gathered, the bartender finally told him to leave me be and asked him to leave the bar.

As he left, I could not help but question my decision to join the military. I was certainly having a very rough start. And little did I know that I would have many difficult times ahead. During my military career, I endured sexual harassment for fear of losing face and losing my job. I also did not want to be known as an informer. My dad always said, "Don't be a rat— you find them at the bottom of the ocean." He must have watched too many Mafia movies, but just the same, I did not want to be a rat! I could handle things myself.

However, I began dreading work because of one officer. In fact, I was having panic attacks about being cornered again. He wanted to flirt and talk about his sex life and what pleased him most. He would often rub up against my body from behind. I knew I had lost all control when he exposed himself to me in the back of the life support shop. I began to believe that I had caused all of this, since not being firm enough was such a problem for me. I hated confrontation, and my insecurity and desire to be accepted left me vulnerable to abuse.

This officer started off as friend in whom I could confide. I shared my innermost secrets about my childhood. I thought I could trust him. I shared my relationship problems with him, including all the arguments and control issues I had been having in my current relationship. And there he was, providing counsel regarding my abusive relationship. I never thought that he would turn out to be no different from the man he convinced me to leave. Once again, more pain and more distrust of men.

Every six weeks a new class would graduate and in came the next. As I was arranging and assigning new lockers and inspecting new pilots' helmets, I noticed a familiar name on the helmet I was scheduled to work on. My stomach flip flopped when I realized it was the "holy roller" from the mountain bike trip! I was nervous, yet excited. I wanted to watch how he acted while flying with us. I thought, *Only a matter of time and he will be like us.* No more praying over food, just drinking and perverted speech! I thought it was sweet that he prayed and loved God, but did I trust him? Are you kidding me! Heck no! He was still a man.

I welcomed him to the squadron, saying, "Good morning, sir. Your equipment is ready for flight." He remembered me from the trip and was quite pleasant, and we made small talk for a bit. Weeks went by, and every time we interacted, he was a gentleman. He would hold the door for me and offer to help me carry parachutes to the life support truck. He even brought me bread from a well-known bakery in town. I thought he wanted what every man wants, but he never made a move! I never heard this man cuss and never once saw him drink!

I wish I could say the same for my behavior. Unfortunately, he saw me drunk, hanging on pilots, and making my way around the officers club for free drinks. In fact, one night, he had to drive me home because I was not able to drive myself (normal night). I was so ashamed of myself because deep down I did not want him to see me that way. I wanted him to see me differently. I realized that night when he took me home that he was not putting on a show, that he was genuine and a man of good moral character. I came to this conclusion because he did not make one move on me! He did not try to spend the night or stay long at all. He made sure I was okay and left.

I ended up having great respect for him and his unshakable faith and character. I had never met anyone like him and I marveled. I was not looking to date this guy, since I had just ended a relationship as did he, but I wanted so desperately to ask him about God and church. I did not have the courage because I thought he would laugh at me. I was on the highway to hell, and he knew it! But eventually as time elapsed, he was so accepting and kind that I finally gathered the courage to ask, "What church do you attend?" and "May I go there, too?" To my surprise, he said, "I go to a small Baptist church, and yes, you may go with me."

Wow! He would not be humiliated meeting me at his church? Hope lightning does not strike! And so we went, and I never did get hit by lightning. In fact, I began to hear about Jesus and I began to ask my new friend all about his God.

Eventually, we said our goodbyes because he was off to Luke Air Force Base for F-16 training. He had become a great friend in those few weeks, and it was hard to say farewell. We were not permitted to date, since he was an officer and I was enlisted, so a relationship was out of the question.

As he left, I realized that a lucky woman out in Arizona was going to marry this amazing man. I was hurt knowing it could never be me. Even if the rules allowed me to date him, I knew it could never be me. I was not like him, and I was not a Bible girl. I was divorced, a drunk, and one of "those" girls. And if you were one of "those" girls, you dated only one of "those" guys. He was far above my caliber and I knew that. I wished him the best and moved on. Or did I?

We remained friends, and he checked in on me. He continued to answer my questions about God and the Bible, and that became a regular phone session. I felt so out of his league, as if I were a biblical idiot, when he would ask me to open my Bible and turn, let's say, to Genesis. *Where is the book of Genesis?* It would take what seemed like hours to find one verse! I was in over my head with this Bible stuff and found myself getting terribly frustrated because I was not getting it!

I confess that once my friend left for Arizona, I never returned to that church we attended in Mississippi. I did keep seeking and asking questions, but was still so angry with God about my past. It was as though my anger for all my losses kept me from believing and accepting Jesus. None of the books in the Bible really spoke to me. I could not understand most of the Bible, I could not relate, and deep down I still criticized and questioned God for my past. However, there was one book in the Bible that I had not yet heard of.

CHAPTER 14
Reading the Book of Job

Who is this that questions my wisdom
with such ignorant words? Brace yourself
like a man, because I have some questions
for you and you must answer them.

—Job 38:2–3

*M*y girlfriend was getting married in Phoenix, and she surprised me by asking me to be in her wedding party. I was honored but also wondered about my Bible teacher and friend. I really missed him and desperately wanted to see him again. I thought about whether we would finish our discussions about God. I was hoping to continue where we had left off, since I admittedly had become very fond of him. I missed him terribly and enjoyed his presence and the peace I felt around him.

As I thought about reuniting with him, I was thrilled and yet scared because I felt an unexplainable connection to him, a connection I had never experienced. And before I knew it, I was in a car with a girlfriend headed to Phoenix, Arizona, to be in a wedding and see him again!

She and I booked a hotel for that week, and I invited my Bible friend to the wedding reception, knowing we could pick up where we left off. My plan was to have him also accompany me at the wedding. I asked if he would be willing to accompany me, and to my delight, he said yes, and so there we were, together again. I was attracted to him and his moral character, but I knew I was not worthy of such a man. However, if only for one night I could pretend I was.

I danced with him, and he looked so handsome. He looked great in his flight suit, too, but this time he was formally dressed and there was no bar smoke. I had only one drink that night because I did not want to ruin the evening by making a fool of myself, at least not on this night. I remember how he looked at me that night. I was wearing a beautiful gown that was simple yet elegant. My hair was up, with loose pieces falling against my neck, and my makeup was professionally done (I looked like I was going to the morgue), but he insisted that I looked beautiful. What an amazing evening.

We had missed each other, though I found it hard to believe that he would miss me. I thought I was just a project for him, since he mainly talked God with me. I remembered thinking of him as a prince or at least thinking if there were such a thing as a prince, he would be what I had envisioned. He was 6 foot 3, dark, and very handsome in his elegant dress clothes. He stood above the rest both physically and morally. He was a man of great integrity; he was honest and true. But mostly, he was a God-fearing man and genuinely loved the Lord. If fairy tales were true, I felt as though I just met one of Disney's finest princes.

As we held hands for our dance, painful thoughts about who I was mocked me. *He is too good for you, Maryann. You will never find a man like him. He would never want you. It is too late for you. Look at your past. You are damaged goods! Don't you dare let him in. If he even knew of your past, he would judge and condemn you just like the rest of those religious people.*

The odds were against me! And, of course, he was an officer and I was enlisted. He could be court marshaled if we were to date. Going to church was one thing, but dating would ruin his career! Like Cinderella when the clock struck midnight, I wanted to run from him in fear he would see how wretched and defiled I really was underneath my outward appearance. My negative thoughts consumed me. The words that I had heard in my abusive relationships tormented me. I had been abused because I deserved it, and no man would ever want me or put up with me, this man especially. I was told this over and over again by a man in my life, and I believed it. The thought of never seeing my friend again calmed my fears, and I knew that this would be our last farewell.

After the wonderful night came to an end, so did our time together. On our last night, he invited me to do a one-on-one Bible study at his apartment. I am not sure why, but I felt compelled to share my upbringing with him. I assumed it would be the last time we saw one another again, so sharing my past would not matter. He lived in Arizona, and I was about to join the Air National Guard in Pennsylvania. So I was brave enough to be transparent with him because I had the safety of knowing it was over anyway. Does that make sense? In my heart, I wanted to push him away, and I knew my past would do the job. A great ending: I scare him away, he runs for the hills with his Bible, damning me to hell, and the story ends.

My plan backfired. He did not run. Instead, he opened the Bible. I was amazed. After all that I shared about my parents not marrying, the abuse, the alcoholism, my mother's mental illness, the divorce, and my own issue with drinking, instead of running away, he felt compelled to stay.

I painfully shared my heart that night. He was a great comfort for me, and he felt safe. To my surprise, he listened to me, and I was not even drunk while telling the story this time. I shared with him how painful it was to bury my father and lose my mom to addiction and mental illness, and I shared my health scare. Then I told him of my divorce. I did not, however, tell him how mad I was at his God. I wanted to respect him. Nevertheless, I felt so safe in sharing and not feeling judged. I boldly told him all things, and yet there he was, not running from the mess that I had just revealed. He had a Bible in hand ready to read the Word yet again to me.

After I dropped the "Maryann's chaotic life" bomb on him, he said, "You know, your story reminds me of a story in the Bible." I thought to myself, *Really? Surely there is not a Maryann story in that Bible! Oh wait, is her name Jezebel? It is a Holy Bible, right?* He said, "Your story reminds me of the book of Job." He asked if I had ever heard of Job. Of course I hadn't. When looking at the title, Job, I thought it said job, as in a place to work job. A job I was for this man, I can say that! I barely knew about Adam and Eve! Did he forget whom he was talking to! "No," I said.

He opened up the Bible to the book of Job. I did not know if he was going to condemn me or cast demons from me. After all, I had just revealed my entire history to him. No, he did not open the Bible to condemn me. He opened it in hopes of redeeming me.

I was curious to see who this Job character was. And so there we were in complete silence. All I could hear were the ruffling sounds of pages moving in the Bible. We sat down and began to read the book of Job together.

Hearing about Job's trials, I marveled because he too had experienced great hardships. As my friend continued to read, I realized that this man Job had lost all his possessions, his children, and his health. His loss was great, just like mine was. Reading Job's story, I could relate to his sorrow. The difference, however, between Job and me was that he was a righteous man and was pleasing in the sight of the Lord, while I was not. Job honored God in everything. Those details alone made me even angrier with God. *Job loved you, God, and this is how you responded. How I question you!* I felt for Job and empathized deeply.

Strangely, as my friend kept reading, the Bible became easy to understand, alive. I am not sure if I was so tuned in because I was listing all of God's faults in the story and looking for an excuse to walk away from Him or because I was captivated by a story so similar to my own. Maybe I was anxiously anticipating how Job would respond to his God. I had tried to read and comprehend the other stories in the Bible, but I just could not relate or could not grasp the wisdom of the Word. But this story was hitting home. My emotions were high, and I was consumed with Job's story.

I was in complete disbelief when I heard what Job did in response to his despair and great loss. His response was quite the opposite of what I had done in my past. Job had just learned about his children being crushed in a building, not just one child, but all of them. He also learned that he had lost his servants and possibly his entire means of survival when all his crops and animals were destroyed!

What would you have done? Shake your fist? Vow to God that you would never serve Him again? Or at least question His existence? Be honest. You may even be in that place with God as you read this book—so hurt and asking Him, "Where were you, God?" But no, that is not what this Job fellow did. The Bible says that Job stood and tore his robe in grief, then he shaved his head and fell to the ground and worshiped God! He said, "I came naked from my mother's womb, and I will be naked when I leave. The Lord gave me what I had, and the Lord has taken it away. Praise the name of the Lord!" (Job 1:21).

Where did he find this desire to worship a God who would permit such devastation? Worshiping a God who would take away our most valuable treasures on earth did not make sense, and I could not comprehend Job's religion or his God, unless this was truly a relationship of sorts. A God who is untouchable and far off is easy to walk away from, but a God offering a relationship and deep intimacy is quite different, and if I did not know better, this Job knew God like a friend.

I was profoundly taken aback by Job's response in praising God. I thought, *He does not deserve our praises. Look what He has done! I will not praise a God who has so viciously taken away my entire family!* My friend kept reading, and my heart was beating fast. I was getting emotionally charged and at the same time so confused by Job. He made no sense logically speaking. His character truly was righteous. But more so, he knew His God in a way that I did not. He was in a relationship, it appeared, and not just any relationship, but an intimate one.

My friend and I at this point were both reading. My eyes would not leave the pages as he read and I followed. Normally when my friend shared the word, I listened out of respect, but not a real desire to understand, but on this night I wanted to know every detail of this man Job's testimony. It grabbed hold of me. Not only was I hearing about Job for the first time, but I was also hearing about a devil who speaks to God. He was the one who asked permission to oppress Job. He was also called the Accuser. I began to consider the possibility that my afflictions too were caused by the Accuser. And if the Devil was real and was truly responsible for my losses, I knew that I was going to go to war with him for all he had done! Had I been warring against God all this time when it was the Accuser who had stolen from me? Was it Satan who had me convinced that God was not real or that God was not worthy of worship?

This book began to reveal a spiritual battle that I had just begun to recognize, a realm that I had not yet known existed. Job 2:1-2 says, "One day the members of the heavenly court came again to present themselves before the Lord, and the Accuser,

Satan, came with them. 'Where have you come from?' the Lord asked Satan. Satan answered the Lord, 'I have been patrolling the earth, watching everything that's going on.'"

I began to realize at that moment that this Accuser is watchful and deliberately patrols, seeking whom he could harm. The Bible says that Satan then struck Job with terrible boils from head to foot. My emotions were beginning to move me, and my fury and my questions about God kept me motivated enough to continue reading. I knew that my last Bible study night with my friend would either end good due to biting my tongue, or end bad once I gave him my opinion about the God in his Bible. Again, it was our last night, and my reputation with him was no longer a concern.

As I read, not only did I relate to Job's pain, but when I read his wife's response to the situation, I thought, *Finally, a woman of wisdom with a response that makes more sense!* There Job was, suffering to the highest degree any man could suffer in my opinion, and there was his wife, a woman with a response that I too would have had.

"Job scraped his skin with a piece of broken pottery as he sat among the ashes. His wife said to him, 'Are you still trying to maintain your integrity? Curse God and die.'" (2:8). I may have said, go drink something honey, and forget about your God!

When she said, "Are you still trying to maintain your integrity?" I thought the same thing. *When is he going to tell His God to go to hell like I had?* She told her husband to curse God and die! I wanted to do the same. Just curse him and die so the pain would go away. This was not just a book to me at the moment; it was my life on paper! This book summed up all my thoughts, my fears, my feelings, my pain, my questions and my anger. For the first time ever, the Bible's words had my undivided attention!

I agreed with Job's wife, but what he said in response to her seemed directly aimed at me. He said, "You foolish woman, should we only accept the good things from the hand of God and never anything bad?" (Job 2:10). My heart sank when Job spoke those words. He was speaking to my heart with great conviction. He was speaking to me! "Maryann, are you going to accept God only for the good and not the bad?"

But I could not at that moment see the good in what God had done. I was blinded by bitterness, pain, and resentment toward God! Have you been there? And just when I thought the book was nearing an end, it began to shake my very being. I was being lectured about areas of my life that only God could address. That secret place was being exposed in the book of Job. I wanted to die the day I sought God in that portrait studio. As Job said, "What I always feared has happened to me. What I dreaded has come true. I have no peace, no quietness; I have no rest, only trouble comes." (Job 3:25-26). Have you ever felt like Job?

Job then questions God and His wisdom. His pain and trials provoked him to question God. Can you relate here? For my entire life, I questioned God. *Where were you, God, when I was a child and desperately sought a prince to rescue me? Why didn't you come for me? When I was under the kitchen table, trembling with Kriste, waiting for the police to respond to another domestic violence call, where were you? When I lost my dad, lost my home, my health? Where were you, God?*

This book ignited a fire within me. Job's words were identical to what I had felt. "My bed will not comfort me, and sleep would not ease my misery. I would rather be strangled- rather die than suffer like this." (7:13-15). But just when I had had enough of Job's story, God began to speak audibly to Job! What? God speaks to people? He doesn't talk to us! Really? I have got to hear this! My friend began to read how God questioned Job. I was not prepared to hear these next verses. God was about to have a one-on-one with me too, and I was not ready to receive what He was about to say to my soul.

We were now reading chapter 38 in which the Lord challenges Job. Well, to my surprise, God was challenging me! The Word came to life, and I could hear God speak to my very core in this passage: "Who is this that questions my wisdom with such ignorant words? Brace yourself like a man, because I have some questions for you, and you must answer them" (Job 38:2-3). It was as though God Almighty pulled up a seat next to me and spoke to my very soul, saying, "Sit down, little girl. It is my turn! Maryann, you have questioned me and my ways your entire life. Now I will question you, and you will need to brace yourself!" I did so with all that I had. I was frantic knowing that Job had to answer God's questions, and at that moment I felt as though I too needed to answer Him.

God asked Job, "Where were you when I laid the foundations of the earth? Tell me if you know so much" (Job 38:4). "Where were you when I laid the foundations of the earth, Maryann? Tell me if you know so much!" Weeping, I continued reading. "Who determined its dimensions and stretched out the surveying line? ... Who kept the sea inside its boundaries?" (38:5-8). I had no answers!

God kept speaking and challenging me in His Word. The more I read the more real and mighty God became to me. He shook me to the core. Then the Lord asked Job, "Do you still want to argue with the Almighty? You are God's critic, but do you have the answers?" (Job 40:2). I too was criticizing God! "Maryann, do you still want to argue with me, the Almighty?" I began to revere God the moment I heard him speak.

I was nearly trembling at this. I had questioned His wisdom and His very ways. I had used human logic to explain God and to mock Him, and I now realized that a human point of view is a trap from Satan (Matt. 16:23). I had no answer in response to God, and my rationalization was puny in comparison with His Word and His ways. I had no words. I was utterly speechless before this mighty God. This book permitted me to see God and feel God in all His glory, power, and might for the very first time.

Job replied to God, "I know that you can do anything, and no one can stop you. You asked, 'Who is this that questions my wisdom with such ignorance?' It is I-and I was talking about things I knew nothing about, things far too wonderful for me. You said, 'Listen and I will speak! I have some questions for you and you must answer them.' I had only heard about you before, but now I have seen you with my own eyes. I take back everything I said. And I sit in the dust with ashes to show my repentance" (Job 42:1-6).

I was moved deeply by God's Word and Job's repentance. I was awestruck and felt great remorse for all I had said and done. My grief over the way in which I had rejected and responded to God was apparent as I said through tears of humility and sorrow, "Lord, forgive me! I blamed you all my life for my sorrows. I did not know you were real. I questioned you, cursed you and sinned. I have sinned greatly against you, and I sit here in despair over the ways in which I criticized the very God who created me. You are the very God who met me in that portrait studio and the very God who would look upon me right now and speak to a woman of great sin and brokenness." I not only was hearing from God, but I felt His Holiness and it was making me tremble. I said, "Lord I have come against you and mocked you most of my life, and yet you speak to me today as though you have always loved me, never left me, and you still pursue me. I don't deserve a God like you to even look upon me and my sin."

I hung my head low. I was utterly convicted for the way I had questioned this great God of mine. Truly I had just fallen in love with a God whom I had only heard about, but on this night I saw Him with my own eyes, I felt Him with my own hands, and His touch was like no other. Like Job said, "forgive me Lord, for I had only heard about you, but today I see you!" (42:5). He became my God and my Father that evening, and I became his daughter, no longer fatherless and desperate for love. He became the love of my life as He so graciously accepted my plea for forgiveness, and His Son became my Savior! Oh my God, how great thou art!

I did not come to Him that night with a burnt sacrifice; I came to Him and offered my broken spirit. I begged Him to remove my brokenness, my stains, and my wounds. *Lord, I am so sorry,* I said to myself. *Forgive me for being so angry with you and for hating you. I need you. I want you. Father, take me just as I am. Will you forgive me? Be my God as you are Job's God. He refused to curse you, and here I am… I've been cursing you most of my life. And I want to love you like Job loves you, and I want you to love me, too.*

I could not contain the tears that ran down my face. There was such a release. I felt light, as though I was floating. A peace that was beyond my understanding. For the first time in my life, I felt free. I let God in that night after keeping Him so distant for so many years. I let Him in, and not only did He come in, but His love in that moment consumed me and transformed my life!

As my friend was preparing to end our Bible study that night, I had accepted Christ as my Savior while reading the book of Job. When Job's wife told him to curse God and die, I wanted to do the same. But amid all his losses and despair, Job refused. He said, "No. My redeemer lives!" I realized that my redeemer lived, too! God spoke to me so powerfully that I wept uncontrollably. Job's story made me realize that God was God. Job had a reverent respect for God and a relationship with Him; even after all his losses, he praised Him, and so there I was, praising Him, too.

That night I felt as though Jesus had begun knocking on the door with each page turning, and the moment I peeked through the door crack, He barged right in and held me tight! Not only did He hold me but He loved me and set me free. I had never felt such love in my entire life! Love consumed me. I had searched so long for this kind of love in all avenues except His, and finally, after waiting my whole life for a rescuer and prince, I found the only rescuer and prince. I found Him and His name is Jesus!

My friend wept with me. I began to weep before him, and I glanced up in hopes that he could explain what was happening to me. He was caught up in what I was feeling and was weeping just as hard as I was. I was instantly transformed! It was as though the very presence of almighty God was in that room with us, and neither one of us could contain our tears or the feeling of such great love. Not only did Christ replace my brokenness, He also delivered me from alcohol that very day. I was made new.

CHAPTER 15

Consumed by His Goodness

After Job had lost everything, God
gave him twice as much.

—Job 42:10

This would be a good time to introduce my friend, the one who ever so patiently took the time to answer all my questions about God, invited me to church, and led me to Christ. His name is Michael McMellon, my husband. I received Christ in June 2000, and we married in August of that year. We did not wait very long, did we? I had so much peace about our marriage that there was no room for fear. It was so apparent that God had a plan.

His plan was far greater than I could ever have imagined. I was a girl who have given up hope of being rescued, restored, and married again—let alone married to an honorable, godly man. This was clearly something only God could see me as worthy of having. I never imagined any of this would come true. But as the Scriptures say, "All things are possible in Christ," and I am here as living proof of that. And the woman who I was no longer existed. I was a new woman in Christ, and so the woman to whom Michael proposed was the new Maryann. "Therefore, if anyone is in Christ, he is a new creation; the old has gone, the new has come!" (2 Cor. 5:17). We were now equally yoked, just as God would have it. The Lord blessed me with an amazing husband. Michael asked for my hand in marriage, and my life has been filled with huge blessings. I will never forget the day he surprised me with an engagement ring. I was living in Pennsylvania when he decided to fly out to spend some time with me. We went to a beautiful place called McConnell's Mill. Once we arrived, Michael was on the hunt for the most appropriate place to ask for my hand in marriage. I had no idea what he was doing! We ventured out deep into the greenery that surrounded us to find a rocky stream with big boulders everywhere. The greenery and the sound of flowing water were captivating. As we bounced from one boulder to the next, he said, "This looks good." I thought we were going to sit down and read our Bibles. However, that was not what he had planned.

God's creation and beauty surrounded us in this sanctuary. As I looked at Michael, he smiled and hugged me tightly. I loved his warm embraces; they were so secure, so pure. After his affectionate embrace, he began to lower himself on the boulder where we were standing. His gaze never left mine. I had no idea that he was going to utter the words I had only wished for, words I never dreamed a man would direct toward a girl like me. As I gazed back at him, I heard him gently say, "Maryann Trainer, will you spend the rest of your life with me?"

Tears welled immediately. I was in disbelief. I threw my hand over my mouth in complete amazement and joy. I thought, *Could this be real?* Just weeks had passed since I had found the love of my life, Christ, and now this? I was so conditioned to bad events, events that promise pain, and now I could not contain the goodness that God was bringing to my life. I wept in gladness; it was as though all the pain from my past was being replaced with great joy!

I paused for a moment to thank God for all He had begun in my life. As Michael patiently awaited my response, I cried and said, "Yes!" At that moment I thought, *God, my God, how great you are to me! Look what you have done for me, Lord! Who am I that you would do this for me?*

The moment Michael knelt to ask for forever with me, God opened up the skies and the rain fell from heaven! Only God would know how much I loved the rain and the smell of rain, and there He was again, loving me like a father who knew his daughter. I cried and we laughed! And the moment Michael stood back up, the rain stopped!

We were so excited about spending forever together! In fact, as we were walking over a covered bridge, we ran into an old couple, and in complete excitement, I blurted out, "We are getting married!" They told us, "Today is our fiftieth wedding anniversary." They were celebrating, too! I will never forget what this older woman did next. She grabbed Michael, gave him a big kiss on the lips, and said, "Congratulations!" I could tell at this moment that Christ had done a work in me, since the old me would have pushed this woman off the bridge for kissing my man! We were a bit shocked, but nonetheless I was so happy that I could have kissed the world, too!

Mike grabbed me by the hand. We were soaking wet, and so we headed back to the car. As if our day were not perfect enough, the sun began to shine, and when we looked at the sky, there was a full rainbow! I can't help but think that our heavenly Father was celebrating with us, since He had completely showed off with rain, a rainbow, and a couple celebrating their fiftieth wedding anniversary! I had never seen a full rainbow! Mike immediately spoke about Noah and how the rainbow in the Bible was symbolic of God's promise. And so it was.

Today I write to you as the mom of two beautiful children, and I am amazed by God! Michael is still one of my greatest treasures. Looking back, I realize that all that was lost has now been recovered. I went from having no prince to meeting the Prince of Peace, being fatherless to having a Father, without a family to a family of four! My tears of joy far exceed my days of sorrow. He not only has blessed me, He has multiplied all that I had lost, just as He did for Job! I am complete now—no more seeking. I am no longer praying for a prince. I found Him in Jesus.

Mike and I renewed our wedding vows in 2009. We eloped and I wanted a wedding! What better place than at Lover's Point, once called Jesus of Lover's point. (Mike Steelman Photography)

My handsome husband… We have been married for almost 12 years! I can't believe you will be in Afghanistan this year on our anniversary. Another part of our story, and we continue to praise God anyway. I love you! (Mike Steelman Photography)

CHAPTER 16

Direct Our Steps, Lord

Trust in the Lord with all your heart and
lean not on your own understanding;
in all your ways submit to him, and
He will make your paths straight.

—Prov. 3:5–6

So there we were, married and stationed in New Mexico where Mike would continue his F-16 fighter career and I would complete college with a degree in psychology. All seemed so blissful at first, but soon our marriage was strained by the lifestyle of a fighter pilot.

Mike loved flying the F-16, and to this day he has fond memories of his time in the jet. But the work environment of a military pilot weighed heavily on him. He didn't fit the mold very well, mainly because he did not hit the bars and drink with his squadron. Mike tried to avoid this lifestyle, and the pressures to conform were a constant drain on him. In fact, our first big argument in marriage came when he failed to return home until four one morning because he was stuck being the designated driver after a night out.

As a new believer and the wife of a fighter pilot, I was struggling with the demands of his squadron, which conflicted with how we chose to honor God. As a former life support technician who had traveled with fighter pilots, I knew firsthand what went on during such trips. I was told, "What goes TDY (temporary duty assignment, AKA business trip) stays TDY." Cheating and sexual insinuations were the norm, and I knew that from experience. However, I was lost back then and quite comfortable with that atmosphere. But this lifestyle worried me to the core now that I was a believer. Mike refused to participate in the bar events, which often degenerated into drunken carousing with vulgarity and pornography, and he found it increasingly difficult to concentrate on his flying proficiency.

His flight commander was not happy that Mike didn't conform, nor was he happy that Mike's flying aptitude was declining. Other pilots told Mike that the only way he would fit with the squadron was to party with them. They would pressure him, saying, "Pilots who get drunk together fight together." This went on long enough that eventually Mike's love of flying for the air force diminished. The joy was sucked right out of him. These demands, coupled with the complicated task of mastering a $30 million supersonic jet, started to consume him. After much prayer, we began to wonder if his days of flying might be limited. The air force wasn't pushing him out, but Mike felt compelled to turn in his wings. We faced so many unknowns, but knew we had to trust the Lord.

The military invests millions in its fighter pilots. We feared that the military could make Mike peel potatoes for the duration of his career to punish him if he were to give up the cockpit. We were anxious on all levels, but knew that God was in control. We would walk in a wide open field with our dog every night, contemplating our decisions. We would look up into the starry sky and feel peace as we wondered about what was happening and what the next steps would be. We wondered how long Mike could keep up with the pace and the pressure. Should he address the issues with his commander? How would he explain his situation? Who would understand his dilemma?

In the early summer heat of Portales, New Mexico, as Mike was flying a dogfight training mission, he had a scare in the jet. With hot air in the cockpit, he was sweating from the maneuvering, and his world began in spin. He felt like he was tumbling, and couldn't focus on the instruments or the heads-up display. For a moment, he did not know whether he was up or down. As quickly as it started, it was over, and he confirmed that his head was spinning, and not the jet.

Foolishly, he told no one and completed the sortie anyway. However, that evening I could tell by his demeanor that something was terribly wrong. I asked if he was okay, and he shared what had happened and how he had had similar experiences in the last few months, though not as intense as this one. He said he had gotten motion sickness at various times during previous missions. I immediately felt ill because I feared the worst. I did not want to lose my husband in a flight mishap. I felt that the squadron was driving him too hard. And now he was getting disoriented and sick in the jet, and we knew that would be the end of his flying career. I wanted it to end sooner rather than later because I feared he would crash.

Soon after, in a discussion with his flight commander, Mike revealed his disorientation issues and his overall dissatisfaction with his career. As they talked, Mike suggested that a change of career out of the cockpit might be in order. For safety purposes and to evaluate his spinning sensations, the air force pulled him from the schedule that week. Mike didn't know that he would never fly an F-16 again.

In short order, the air force sent Mike to flight medicine specialists for physical and psychological evaluations. Thankfully, they found nothing wrong with him, other than the fact that he was generally stressed and worn out. We joked about the psychological tests administered to him, guessing that the doctors thought he must be out of his mind to want to turn in his wings. After all, he was flying one of the best jets in the world and a career as an air force pilot was among the top military aspirations. But Mike knew that flying a jet was not the pinnacle. He knew that it was better to lay down worldly goals in obedience. Surprisingly, the Air Force offered to let him return to the F-16. However, he had lost all heart for it at that point. He respectfully declined, then waited for the penalty. But the penalty never came.

Mike was disqualified from flying, but the air force never removed his wings. Instead, the military asked, "What do you want to do, and where to you want to go?" God blessed us with a new career in Air Force acquisition management. And as the Lord would have it, we were stationed in the very location we had prayed for. Mike was now flying a desk, and though it wasn't exactly glamorous, he was home every night, and the work environment was the polar opposite. Praise God that our challenge was over! Our next challenge was parenting. Not only were we about to venture off into parenthood and face new demands—such as colic, engorged milk glands, stretch marks, not being able to sit and eat, diaper rash, and lack of sleep—but we were about to learn some things that were not part of the *Babywise* manual! I have to admit that basic training was far easier for me than being a mom at first, but the opposition that we were about to endure from the Enemy made basic training and our simulated war tactics look elementary.

CHAPTER 17

Fierce Opposition

For our struggle is not against flesh and
blood, but against the rulers, against
the authorities, against the powers of
this dark world and against the spiritual
forces of evil in the heavenly realms.

—Eph. 6:12

At the beginning of this book, I noted that we have an
enemy. I did not know we had a real enemy until I met
my Prince. And just as a fairy tale would have it, there is a dragon,
and his name is Satan. The Bible says, "And the great dragon was
thrown down, that ancient serpent, who is called the devil and
Satan, the deceiver of the whole world" (Rev. 12:9). Except this is
no fairy tale! The Bible says that we battle not against flesh and
blood, but against principalities and rulers of the unseen world. In
our new season of life as parents, we were about to learn in great
depth what that truly meant.

Life was amazing; God blessed our marriage and Michael's
military career. We seemed to have it all together. We had a healthy
baby girl, we bought our first home, and we were expecting yet
again, and this time it was a boy! A fairy tale of sorts is what
we seemed to be living. However, in all of our blessings and joy,

there came a thief in the night, one who intended to steal from us and destroy us. His name was Satan. Mike and I were about to be introduced to a spiritual realm that is as real as you are. It is a realm of powers and darkness, the unseen world. We were fighting something that we could feel but not see. We were in an all-out war, battling for our minds and our marriage. And Satan also planned on winning our generations to come.

Not long after the birth of Jacob, our second child, I began to experience a battle in my mind. My thoughts were not my own. They were intrusive and unwanted. Some were violent, some were perverted, and I had no control over these repulsive thoughts. They would frighten me and eventually cause despair, panic attacks, and loss of desire to press on. As you know, my mother was mentally ill with paranoid schizophrenia and bipolar disorder. I instantly feared losing my mind and my children. Worse, what if I hurt them?

Ashley was twenty-seven months and Jacob was ten months old when my mind seemed to have been hijacked. I was so stricken with anxiety and panic attacks that the mere thought of making them so much as a bowl of cereal was completely overwhelming.

I was stuck in a fight-or-flight mode and I was burning out fast. I knew that I should have been checked into a mental ward, but I was afraid of that, too. I feared losing my children and my husband. I could not even read the Bible. The words filled me with anxiety and fear, especially if I read about violence or murder. I was robbed of all that I had: my God, my children, the ability to worship, and my husband. I was afraid of him as well. I had bizarre thoughts of Michael harming the children and leaving me.

Guilt and condemnation from my past also caused me depression; suddenly, I was a whore and unworthy of Michael. I was a prisoner of my mind and could not prevent the tormenting thoughts. No matter where I went, my mind followed me, and there was no escape. I even had thoughts of suicide but was too afraid to follow through. Fear consumed me, and I began to isolate myself. I could no longer enjoy life. I even hated eating. I remember having to make myself eat so I would not lose any more weight. I sought help from a medical doctor, and he offered me an antidepressant, which I took. The side effects were horrible. It made my mind race. I vomited every morning and had horrible stomach issues from the medication. Basically, I added vomiting and irritable bowel syndrome to my plethora of problems. I had no idea why I was being tormented by my own mind, and nothing was helping me, not the Bible, not church, not medicine.

I was even being tormented in my sleep, with dreams of demons and sexual perversion. One dream was so intense that I awoke sweating. I dreamed that I was walking up the stairs to enter our bonus room, where we had our office, and when I tried to get up those stairs, a monstrous form of a man jumped on me and wrestled me to the ground. It was so powerful that I could barely call out the name of Jesus. This thing had me, and I seemed powerless. Though it was a dream, it consumed my thoughts. So where does one go, tormented awake and tormented while asleep? God help me!

After praying for a revelation from God and for healing, God would speak and reveal the source of my problem. Not by coincidence, at church that Sunday, the sermon was on pornography. The pastor said he needed to have his wife control the TV with a code, placing boundaries to guard his heart from lust and prevent him from stumbling.

That sermon really spoke to me because I saw pornographic images at age five. In fact, I still have "pop-ups" from the pictures that I saw as a child and later in adulthood. Those images scarred me as a young woman because I thought I had to look like that to be attractive. The pastor's sermon about pornography made me realize that even the church battles this. In my spiritually immature mind, I assumed that Christians were free from all failings and that we would not struggle because we have Jesus and have been set free. But what I did not know is that even though we are free, that does not mean we are free from the Enemy. The Bible says, "He roams the earth seeking whom he can devour." (1 Peter 5:8).

After this great Sunday service, I sensed the need to ask Michael about the sermon. I felt pressure from within to ask questions I really did not want answered. I had believed from the beginning that since Michael had led me to Christ he was perfect; he was not a man like my dad, and I would *never* have to fret about him stumbling in the area of pornography. To me, he was nearly as high as God, and how many of you know that God does not share His throne? There is only one perfect man, and I was about to find that out through complete devastation.

As we lay in our master bedroom after church, I decided to explore a bit. The Holy Spirit would not let up. I asked, "So what did you think about the message?" He said, "It was fine." I thought, *Okay that is good enough. No more questions.* But then I heard in my spirit, *Ask him if he has ever seen pornography.* So I asked, and he said he had. I began to rationalize his answer. *Of course he has seen pornography. He worked in a fighter squadron. But now we have this new life, a family life, a home with children, and we fear God. See, all is well!* Oh, but God was not finished!

I heard again in my spirit, *I want you to ask Michael the last time he viewed pornography.* I was very frustrated because I knew that if his answer was not what I wanted to hear, I would be shattered. With great bravery, I asked, and his answer pierced me with great affliction.

Michael revealed his most recent computer incident, and as he told me about clicking on a pop-up website, I felt as though something in me had just died. Trust, security, self-worth, self-esteem, self-image, and nearly my faith in God had been shaken by his response. *He was supposed to be a Christian! He is no different than my daddy!*

Not only did I beat him up for this moral failure, but I beat myself up for not being able to meet his needs. My thoughts raced. *I am unattractive; I need to lose weight and have surgery.* I thought maybe if I looked like those women on the computer, it would be enough for him and he would never go outside of our marriage again. He may not have had a physical affair, but just the same, he went outside of our marriage for sexual pleasure, and the pain was unbearable. I thought, *God help me I am falling apart in great anger and pain. I am confused and I have no place to run. I have two children, and how can I take care of them if I leave?*

Ladies reading this book, I know many of you may have experienced this, and I am so sorry. If you are crying, I wish I could hug you, but I am here to tell you that Satan had made his way into our marriage by tempting my husband with pornography, and my flesh wanted to seek vengeance! I wanted to hurt him or betray him the way he betrayed me! I was so scared to see my old flesh life rise up in me. I wanted to leave him, drink, and get reassurance from someone else. In fact, I decided to hit the gym and be perfect physically so I would never have to endure such pain again. Girls, I know some of you have been here, and I am going to share a life lesson with you that I pray will prevent you from falling into the pit I just described.

I began working out and losing weight. I was looking good and feeling good. In fact, as Satan would have it, I was drawing more glances than ever. And in my brokenness, I craved that attention. Eventually, a workout instructor took a special interest in me, and boy was I vulnerable. I had so much anger for my husband that hurting him was a goal! After a long, hard workout, this instructor asked if we could start meeting there and working out together.

I knew he wanted more than that, he wanted me, and I wanted to be wanted. I said, "Sure," but when he asked me for my phone number, as clear as these words are that you are reading, I heard, "Maryann, I know you are angry with Michael, and I know you want to hurt him, but in doing so, you will be hurting me. Why would you do that to me?"

I put the pen down, handed the instructor his paper, and ran out of that gym never to return. I sat in my car and wept. *Lord, I am depressed. I feel as though I am losing the battle. I am riddled with depression and I am numb. What is this, Lord? Why us? Have I not experienced enough, Lord? Oh, but I love you and I never want to hurt you, Lord! Not after what you have done for me, but help me fight this and win. Please forgive me for wanting to seek vengeance, but promise me that this pain will flee from me.*

Michael began to confess his moral failure in our marriage. He shared even more with me. He said that on a business trip he set his alarm to watch an inappropriate movie, and when the alarm went off, he went to the bathroom where for the first time he heard the audible voice of God. The voice said, "Michael, if you watch that, I will kill you." In tears, Mike lamented that of all the things he could have heard from his heavenly Father, he had to hear that.

Mike was broken and in despair, as was I. We felt as though there was a great weight on us. He was concerned about my depression and anxiety, and I was concerned about our marriage. It felt as though he had had an affair. My image was shattered into a thousand pieces, and I had no idea how to be restored. I also felt as though I deserved what had happened. And as Satan would have it, a church leader informed me that the sexual sins of my past were sins against my husband. His words pierced me, and I thought, *Take my life now, Lord, please! I can't bare this shame and blame.*

After at least six months of suffering with this guilt and blame for my past sins, the Lord awoke me one morning and called me into my closet. This had been our meeting place. I would try to hear from God but couldn't. During this season of great sorrow, I would lie on the floor of my closet and lay my face on the Bible as tears collected on the pages. But on this day, my tears would no longer fall on those pages, and His Word would no longer be silent. The Lord had decided that I had suffered long enough in my shame, and on this morning He spoke.

As I lay there in the stillness of my closet, repenting yet again to the Lord for my past sins, I asked, "When, Lord, will I be released from my shameful past? When, Lord, will I be delivered from this torment? If I have truly sinned against my husband with the men of my past, how could Michael forgive me?"

In my spirit, I heard the Lord say, "Maryann, I want you to look at your shoes." *What, Lord! You are asking me to look at my shoes at a time like this!* They were lined up in orderly fashion (which in not normal for me), and I heard Him say in my spirit, "Maryann, notice your shoes. Look at them carefully. Do you notice the old pair of shoes you once wore before you met me?" I said to myself, *Oh God, how can I forget!* Then I heard Him say, "I remember what you did in those shoes, Maryann."

As I glanced at those shoes, I remembered how I had soiled them in the clubs with booze and maybe even vomit. I served Satan in those shoes. I was promiscuous in those shoes. I thought, *Why, Lord, are you reminding me again of my past? I am tormented enough, Lord! Don't make me look at my shoes. Father, I am consumed with shame.*

Then I heard Him say, "Maryann, my beloved, do you see the new pair of shoes placed next to the old pair? I placed them there for you. They are new, just like you! I am asking you to walk in those shoes now. You are no longer a part of those old shoes. It is time to get up off this floor and walk in the new shoes and to the new places I am calling you. Now brush yourself off and dispose of those old shoes; start walking and talking like my beloved child! You, Maryann, are made new. I set you free, and whom my Son sets free they are free indeed (John 8:36)! All things passed away, all things made new, you are new!" (2 Cor. 5:17).

I was reminded that I had been made new, and another chain fell from me that day. The Lord renewed my strength, and I could hear from Him again! The Lord knew I needed to be strengthened for the battle that was ahead, but I was about to fight it wearing new shoes! Maybe it is time that you walk in new shoes as well! Maybe some combat boots? Are you with me?

It was three in the morning, and Mike and I awoke to a piercing wail from our daughter's bedroom. She was two years old and screaming a scream that I had never heard before. As a mother, I knew something was wrong. I flipped on the bedroom light and saw that she had a look of terror on her little face. I asked her what was wrong and she said that a large monkey with a long tail had tried to jump on her and get into her bed. As the hair stood up on the backs of our necks, she described what seemed to be a devil or demon. She finally calmed down and slept with us that morning. Mike and I admitted to each other that her description was terrifying, and we knew she was not dreaming.

A few nights later, Mike was awakened. He saw what seemed to be a black shadow with the form of a man. He was startled, and just as quickly as he saw it, this thing moved like lightning and jumped on him. It began to wrestle with him. He described holding the right arm of this blackness as it tried to get into his nose, mouth, and eyes. Mike rebuked it and it fled.

By the next morning, we knew we had something greater to fight in our home. We no longer faced just a fight for our marriage and a fight for my mental health. We had permitted this spirit in our home, and Mike knew the door to darkness was opened because of pornography. Not only was I suffering with perverted thoughts and dreams, but now this spirit was going after the entire household, including my daughter!

We both sensed God calling us to pray through the rooms of our home and rebuke anything that was not of God, telling it to leave in Jesus' name. Strangely, the bonus room where the computer was located was the last room in which we prayed. When we entered that room and stood before that computer, Mike and I felt God's presence and power as though we were on fire. It was clear where this demon came from: he entered our home after Mike opened the door of pornography, and our entire family was being tormented! But in the power and name of Jesus we rebuked that spirit, and our house was full of peace again.

Looking back, I realize that the moment I was saved by Christ my prince, a war began for my head, my family, and my children. Little did I know that these experiences were part of my calling and my ministry. God was showing us how to war and what doing this looked like. I had no idea that the battle could be so fearsome and brutal and nearly mean my defeat. During those days, I was beaten, battered, and bruised by the Enemy. I recalled that in the book of Job, Satan told God that he had been busy patrolling the earth. The revelation that Satan was patrolling the earth and stirring up evil as a way to end my marriage, and the future of my children and generations to come, made me furious. But God has taken the pain that Satan inflicted on our family, turned it around, and is using it for His kingdom.

You may be in a place where you feel completely destroyed, battered, and bruised, but I am here to tell you that the King of Abraham, Isaac, and Jacob can use your circumstance for His glory. Please don't let your circumstance at this moment determine your faith. I did not, and I am about to share with you a part of my life that I thought would be my ruin. Little did I know that my next step in spiritual growth would affect me and my suppositions for the rest of my life. I will quote Matthew 12:29: "For who is powerful enough to enter the house of a strong man like Satan and plunder his goods? Only someone even stronger—someone who could tie him up and then plunder his house." I was about to learn that Christ Jesus is the stronger one, and my Lord was going to show me how to tie up my Enemy!

CHAPTER 18

Forgiveness

I command you this, to love
others as I have loved you.

—John 15:12

*D*ear sister in Christ, if you have experienced the betrayal of a husband looking at pornography, I want to take a moment to say that I am so sorry. I know the pain. I know how this situation shatters us in many ways. It can be completely destructive to our spirits and our minds. There is no doubt that pornography is a tool from Satan. But what is more destructive is unforgiveness. When we choose not to forgive an offense, it is as though we are drinking the poison, yet another great trap from the Evil One.

I did not trust my husband for years after this offense. In fact, the way in which I handled it was a great sin. Instead of warring for my husband against the kingdom of darkness, I joined with Satan by coming into agreement with him. Mike was already being condemned by the Enemy. His guilt consumed him, and my comments were daggers directed toward him instead of Satan.

Girls, when our husbands are thrown into a war, when they are in a fierce battle, it is not the right time to side with Satan. You need to war for your husband, not against him! Speak life and not death into your marriage. I learned this the hard way. The longer I delayed forgiving my husband, the longer Satan resided and tormented us. We must accept what God says about our men! Speak life and stop expending so much energy on the darkness. We need to try praying and speaking the Scripture over our husbands instead of cursing them. If you saw your husband wounded in a bloody battle, would you sneer at him and remind him of all his failures, or would you help save him? I suggest you do what Christ did for you: war for him with your life and never give up! I am by no means asking you to stay in an abusive position, seek shelter and a counselor. Christ did not call us to be victimized. However, he also did not call us it be cowards and quit. Many marriages could have been restored if Christ was center, and warring was executed accurately.

The moral failure in our marriage tormented me in our bedroom, in the way I looked and the way I performed. I knew I could never measure up to the images Mike had watched. But one day, I realized that I was comparing myself to a whore and not to a daughter of a King. I became free from more bondage that day as I realized I was trying to live up to the Evil One's standards and not God's standards for a daughter.

Our bedrooms with our spouses are meant to be holy places. Satan wants to pervert and rob the sons and daughters of the King in this area. Well, God set me straight. I am the daughter of a King, and I refuse to view myself in any other way.

Not only did I have to know my position as a King's daughter, but the Lord showed me that I needed to forgive like one. I permitted bitterness and unforgiveness to permeate my entire being. I was held captive by these feelings. How the Enemy loved to watch me walk around completely chained by unforgiveness and bitterness! They choked my spirit, and the weight was preventing me from walking in victory. But God was about to have words with me, and in the love of a Father's gentle correction, I was set free. During my devotion time, the Lord took me to the parable of the unforgiving debtor, and for those of you who have not heard it, let me share.

Therefore, the kingdom of heaven is like a king who wanted to settle accounts with his servants. As he began the settlement, a man who owed him ten thousand bags of gold was brought to him. Since he was not able to pay, the master ordered that he and his wife and his children and all that he had be sold to repay the debt.

At this the servant fell on his knees before him. "Be patient with me," he begged, "and I will pay back everything." The servant's master took pity on him, canceled the debt and let him go.

But when that servant went out, he found one of his fellow servants who owed him a hundred silver coins. He grabbed him and began to choke him. "Pay back what you owe me!" he demanded.

His fellow servant fell to his knees and begged him, "Be patient with me, and I will pay it back."

But he refused. Instead, he went off and had the man thrown into prison until he could pay the debt. When the other servants saw what had happened, they were outraged and went and told their master everything that had happened.

Then the master called the servant in. "You wicked servant," he said, "I canceled all that debt of yours because you begged me to. Shouldn't you have had mercy on your fellow servant just as I had on you?" In anger his master handed him over to the jailers to be tortured, until he should pay back all he owed.

This is how my heavenly Father will treat each of you unless you forgive your brother or sister from your heart.

—Matt. 18:21–35

The meaning of this parable was undeniable: my unforgiveness made me that wicked servant! I know what debt my King erased from my life! How about you? I may not have stumbled in the area of pornography, but I have in the areas of pride, lust, greed, and blatant unforgiveness. And to refuse to set my debtor free from his debts, after all I had been pardoned for, was wicked! In the area of debt (an offense by another), we need to be reminded that we were in great debt to our King. Our sins were our debt, and I have yet to meet a greater sinner than myself. My King went to the cross to pay my debt (a large sum, too). I strongly suggest that instead of holding others to pay the price, you set them free and rejoice that your King has pardoned you, too. Thus another door closed to the Evil One.

The moment I released my husband from his debt, God began to move. And what Satan intended for evil, God is using for our good. The Lord is now using us in the lives of other couples to mentor and share our story in hopes that they do not fall into the same trap. Mike and I know who set our trap (Satan), and we are happy to use this trial to help others avoid the same trap. Because of this experience in our marriage, we have become stronger and closer. I am so proud of my husband. He is truly my best friend.

Recently I have seen God do a great work in my husband regarding areas of temptation. I will never forget one particular day when he approached me in my office in complete vulnerability, saying, "I am struggling with lust. Would you pray for me?" In that moment, it was so clear that God had healed me. Instead of condemning, accusing, and throwing a pity party, I rose to his request and became his prayer warrior. Had I responded any other way, I would have opened a door for Satan to torment our marriage. Coming into agreement with Satan rather than with the Lord is a sin and a failure to war. If we are commissioned by God for His army, we are called to be war heroes who will rescue the flock, not shoot it! Whose side am I on in this war? It had best be my husband's!

I glorified the Lord that day by warring for Him and not warring against Him. No glory to Satan! I was angry, but my anger was not directed toward my husband, but toward Satan. When my husband said he was concerned that his struggle against lust would interfere with his relationship with God, I wept. God revealed to me so much that day. I saw a husband who was hurt about failing in the eyes of his King. Michael did not say, "I am concerned about how this temptation could affect my wife or kids." No, he put God first! He said, "I am worried about how this will affect my relationship with God." When a man puts his God above all things, he is putting his family first! It is a principle that never fails.

That night I prayed over him and rebuked Satan. I went to battle for Mike with God's Word, which is sharper than any two-edged sword. I drew my sword, the Word of God, and in the name of Jesus, I rebuked Satan for what he was trying to do to our family and our marriage. The next morning I spoke to Mike at work and asked how he was feeling, and he said that he was free and no longer being tormented. When darkness is brought into light, it loses its power. Glory to God, we have been given the sword of the Spirit and it is time to use it! What are we waiting for and what are we fighting for? Could it be the generations to come?

CHAPTER 19
Reuniting with Mom

He casts out the evil spirits with a simple
command, and he healed the sick ... He took
our sickness and removed our diseases.

—Matt. 8:16–17

The proceeding chapters have detailed our introduction to
Warfare 101. I realized that Satan had tried to devour us.
But as Christ would have it, His blood covered us and His great
name freed us.

This experience made me dive into the Word to learn how to
fight. When I began to read about Satan, I realized how much he
had stolen from me, not just in my marriage but in my childhood,
and I got angry! I also realized that my mom's mental state was
a result of demonic influence. After studying Neil Anderson's
Victory over the Darkness, I realized that my mom's struggles were
partially due to being involved with the occult. We played with
Ouija boards, tarot cards, and palm reading, and she actually had
a witch friend named Crystal.

I had no idea that those things could still have a hold on
me and my Mom. She eventually ended up on drugs, lived on
the streets for a few years, and survived by selling her body. She
refused to get help after her breakdown. I did not see her for nearly

fourteen years. There were moments when I missed her greatly. I remember the nights I would weep for her and fear that she was dead. But her illness ruled her, and after all my research, I began seeing that illness in a different light. I am not saying that all mental illness is demonic, but I believe that one should explore the spiritual realm first.

When Mom would randomly call me for money, I would try to share the Word of God with her, and when I did, she would breathe heavily and curse God's name with great vulgarity. Yes, she was intoxicated, but it was clear that Satan was using her as a mouthpiece. She also believed that her boyfriend was Jesus. Why does mental illness most often involve negative voices; scary hallucinations, mostly demonic; images and thoughts that torment people, and blatant curses directed against Jesus, never against Buddha or Muhammad? Sounds like the Enemy to me.

Mom was eventually charged with prostitution. She needed money to live and to continue her way of self-medicating. I was losing my mom to the Evil One. Just as he had come for my head, I knew he had hers. As I watched and prayed for my mom, there was a passionate fire stirring in me to war for her. I wanted to snatch her from the oppressor's teeth and put a fierce muzzle around his mouth for Mom and my entire generation. And I knew the only way to conquer this Enemy was Christ.

I so desperately wanted to hold her again. I feared that she would die, and I would never have the opportunity to share Christ with her. I would often pray that God would send a chosen servant to help her. In the midnight hours on my birthday, Christmas, Thanksgiving, and all other family holidays, I would ask God to take care of her. I would ask Him to protect her and provide food. I trusted God and knew He was the only one who could rescue her.

On some nights, the fear and pain from missing a mother's warm embrace nearly consumed me. I had questioned God so much in my past and realized that questioning Him was not the same as believing in Him. My "Why, God?" had become "Okay, God, I will wait on you. But Lord, while I am waiting in fear and yearning for the comfort and love of a mother, would you be that for me tonight?" Every time I have asked Him to love me, He has. The Lord's arms have no equal, and I was comforted in those midnight hours. I believe that He was providing comfort for Mom, too.

God is God and His mighty arm stretches over His sheep. The Bible says, "God has set apart the godly for himself and He will hear them when they call" (Ps. 4:3). He hears us when we call! I don't know you or your circumstance, but I do know my God and I can without reservation tell you that He is mighty! When we seek God, we need to brace ourselves because the God of Abraham, Isaac, and Jacob is about to move!

Have you ever been in a place where you had to leave everything in the hands of God? Have you ever felt that the wait had been long enough? I was in that place. But God's timing is perfect! He showed up in the last hour, and after fourteen years of not seeing my mother and of fearing her dead, I received a phone call from a woman in Sarasota, Florida, that changed my life. She worked for a homeless shelter called the Resurrection House. I was not prepared for this call.

When I picked up the phone, I heard a sweet voice say, "Hello, my name is Vicki. Are you Linda's daughter?" I braced myself as my heart began to palpitate out of my chest. *Oh God, please be with me!* I said, "Yes, I am." She said, "I have your mom; she is in our homeless shelter."

Vicki said she had no idea until recently that Mom even had children. She said that Mom was in rough shape. As I listened to this woman describe my mother's frail, malnourished body, I wept. And Mom's mental illness had even the other homeless people afraid of her. Vicki said that Mom had been dropped off at the shelter and looked like a bag of bones. Mom was so soiled that she was afraid to take a shower. She had been beaten up several times for her money and was in the worst shape imaginable. The pain that I felt upon hearing that Mom had been beaten was unbearable. I tried desperately to hold myself together but failed as my emotions consumed me. I wanted to jump through the phone and keep her safe from harm. However, the weight of what I had just heard did not diminish how grateful I was that Mom was alive.

Vicki said she had to get into the shower with Mom so that she would not be afraid. As she offered such details, I could not help but cry my heart out. I thought, *God help me not to be angry with you, and don't let my emotions consume me.* But in hearing all that this woman had done for Mom, I was left in complete awe. Through all my tears, this stranger became a hero to me because she was taking care of a woman rejected by society, an outcast. Mom was harsh, barely kept her clothes on, and used repulsive language. And yet this woman was not bothered at all by Mom's appearance or speech.

When I could catch my breath and stop crying, I told Vicki that she had blessed me more than words could say. I said, "I don't know if you are a believer, Vicki, but I want you to know that God is going to bless you for what you have done!"

What she said next was undeniable evidence that God had heard and answered all my prayers for Mom. Vicki said, "Oh, sweetheart, God has already blessed me, and yes I am a believer!" How great is our God? As I write this, I am overwhelmed by Him.

After a couple of months of checking in with Vicki, I knew God had opened a door for me to fly to Sarasota and see my mom. I can't tell you how scared I was to go. I had not seen Mom in nearly fourteen years, and that is a long time. But there was no denying that God had made a way where there had seemed to be none, and I needed to go by faith and not fear.

I realized that I would soon have to go to Florida alone. Mike needed to watch the kids, and my sister was going through a hard trial of her own. I was not comfortable with the thought of going alone because I did not know how I would do emotionally. In fact, I did not know if Mom's living conditions were safe. But God assigned a dear friend, Sheri Munshi, to join me. I never asked her to go, but she called me in tears, saying, "I don't know if this is selfish or what, but I can't let you do this alone. Please let me go with you."

As I listened to a friend in tears asking if she could accompany me, I wept again because I could clearly see that God had arranged this reunion in every detail. I was stunned because Sheri is a very busy mom of two and I could not pay her airfare. But she was so adamant that I knew it was God at work. So there we were, buying our tickets to Sarasota where I would embrace my mom after long years of waiting.

Not only did I want to hold my mom again, but I wanted to war for her. I knew in my spirit that God was calling me to witness to her and bring her into His kingdom. I was not going to visit my mom just for a reunion. I knew I would have to fight for Mom and battle the Enemy. The last time I had seen Mom, I was in chains myself, completely consumed by the Evil One, lost without a Savior. But now I was going as a bride of Christ, a daughter of a King, and the power of His Word would be my weapon. Not only did I bring my Bible, but I brought praise music, knowing that Mom and I could worship together. "Amazing Grace" was the song of choice because I could not think of a better song to sing to Christ at this moment of my life.

After a two-hour flight to Sarasota, Sheri and I arrived at Mom's motel. It was there that I met this woman of God named Vicki, the one responsible for reuniting me with my mother and the one who had been caring for her. She helped orchestrate this meeting. When I arrived at the motel, Vicki approached me first and hugged me. In her embrace, I thought, *This is the woman I had been praying would come to the aid of my mom.* I recalled asking God, "Send a servant who belongs to you, Lord, one who could love Mom with Christ," and there I was, embracing the woman God had assigned to Mom.

After embracing Vicki, I looked behind her to see a woman whom I knew in my heart but would not have recognized on the street. Mom had aged beyond her years, her teeth were missing, and her hair was gray. She looked homeless. Her nails were overgrown, her face had straggly hairs on it, and she was very thin. However, that did not deter me from embracing her with great tears of joy. As I walked over to her and hugged her tightly, I thought to myself, *My God, you are so good to me. Only your hand could have given me this day.*

After our embrace, Mom looked at me, and when her gaze met mine, she fell apart weeping. She was in complete disbelief. There I was all grown up at thirty-four, and when she told me how beautiful I was, those words were like salve to my wounds. I thought, *She approves of me!* But sadness also crept in as I saw a woman filled with so much sorrow that I began grieving for her. What was so incredible was the love that I felt for Mom. I was without bitterness or resentment regardless of the past and its wounds. There stood my mom—my mom! And my gratefulness for having her in my arms that day left no room for resentment, just pure thanksgiving. I held her and cried while praising God once again for His greatness. He is faithful!

Sheri and I took Mom back to the Hyatt where we were staying. I wanted to take Mom on a shopping spree and was thrilled to do so. We went to Target where she tried on many different clothes. I watched her get excited over everything. When I took Mom to the dressing room, I noticed that her undergarments were soiled and had holes everywhere. I had to keep my emotions in check. After watching her try on clothes, the next step from what I could see was new bras and panties! We even decided to dye her hair and do her makeup!

Mom and I felt like mother and daughter, and I was so blessed by that. The hardest part was watching people stare at Mom. I thought, *Sure, Mom wears her sins on the outside, but you are no different on the inside.* I found myself getting upset with each gaze, but I was not going to let people steal my joy, so Mom, Sheri, and I hit the pool and the hot tub and celebrated our short time together at the Hyatt.

There were two choices I could have made regarding this event. I could have been angry with God for her condition; I could have grumbled and complained, blamed God, or felt sorry for myself. I am sure that had I glanced around Target, I would have seen a mother and daughter shopping and engaged in normal conversation and could have compared that mom to my mom. I am quite sure I was the only one in the store buying clothes for a homeless mom.

However, when you look for God, you see Him, and when you praise God, you feel Him, and when you show faith in Him, He moves! I may not have "that kind of mom," but I have a mom! And I love her! She may not remember my birthday or be there when I am sick or giving birth to babies, but when you are stripped of all the big things, you begin to appreciate the little things. I was with my mom, and she was alive. So instead of grumbling or complaining, I rejoiced! And when we rejoice in what seems to look pitiful that is called having faith! And it is our faith that moves God, and God was about to move! My mustard-seed faith was about to produce a harvest! Anger harvests bitterness, resentment, and unforgiveness and chokes the Spirit of God, but faith harvests hope, joy, love, and much fruit, brings forth power in the Spirit, and gives glory to our King. Let us choose faith!

After a great night with Mom, we went back to the room to play worship music. Mom had not drunk much, maybe a can of beer, which was miraculous. Her mind was there, which also was amazing, since she had been so disillusioned at times. As I played the song "Amazing Grace," we held hands and sang together. You know the words.

> Amazing grace, how sweet the sound
> That saved a wretch like me.
> I once was lost but now am found,
> Was blind, but now I see.
> T'was grace that taught
> My heart to fear
> And grace my fears relieved.
> How precious did that grace appear
> The hour I first believed.
> Through many dangers, toils and snares
> We have already come.
> T'was grace that brought us safe thus far
> And grace will lead us home.
> The Lord has promised good to me.
> His word my hope secures.
> He will my shield and portion be
> As long as life endures.
> When we've been here ten thousand years,

Bright shining as the sun,
We've no less days to sing God's praise
Then when we've first begun.
Amazing grace, how sweet the sound
That saved a wretch like me.
I once was lost but now am found,
Was blind, but now I see.

I had not heard my Mom sing to me since I was a child, and now here we were holding hands, singing "Amazing Grace." I felt as though I was in heaven! After the song was finished, in my weeping I felt God nudging me to ask Mom if she wanted this God who had rescued me to rescue her. I asked Mom if she wanted Christ to restore her life. When Mom answered yes, it was quite clear why God had sent me to see her.

As I laid my hands on her and led her into the prayer of salvation, I felt the Holy Spirit come over us. As Mom repeated, "Lord Jesus, come into my life and forgive me for my sins," she began to sob, as did Sheri and I. I knew the moment that Mom was moved to tears Christ had met her. I will never forget that moment, and I will never cease to praise God for the reassurance that one day I will see her again in eternity. Thank you, Lord!

Since that day, Mom has been off the streets. She has a long way to go, but I now know she is no longer battling the Enemy alone. She has Christ and the sword of the Spirit. And the way I see it, His Word and Spirit are weapons of mass destruction, making Satan look like a worm with a squirt gun. We need not be afraid of him; he needs to be afraid of us.

CHAPTER 20

A Reflection of God's Hand

"For I know the plans I have for you," declares
the Lord, "plans to prosper you, not to harm
you, plans to give you a hope and a future."

—Jer. 29:11

I have been writing this book since Father's Day. I hope that
you have been able to see the hand of God through my
transparency. And I pray that this book has encouraged you. How
can we not be encouraged by the hand of the Lord?

Looking back, I see myself as a child abducted, then held
captive by Satan for nearly twenty-three years. I see a girl
who was abused by the Evil One. I was beaten, battered, and
bruised, hoping a prince would save me. I had no knowledge
that I was in a war for my soul. Nor did I know that I was
being brainwashed by the lies of the Enemy. When I grew up,
my anger was directed toward God and not the abductor, the
Evil One who came to steal and destroy me. It was not until my
Prince rescued me from darkness that the war and my abductor
were revealed.

The beauty of my story is how what Satan meant for evil
God has turned around and is using for good. I had no idea
that God could take my shame and use it to glorify His name.

I can honestly say that despite all the loss and pain I have experienced, I would not change a thing. If one person goes to the cross, finds Jesus and is set free, my past has meaning and purpose.

I am wondering if that person is you. Are you tired of fighting the war alone? Do you need strength? Do you want to win the war? Are you ready to surrender your life to the cross? If you want to war with me, and war for your family and the generations to come, you need Christ to win the victory. If you are ready to join God's army and be set free as I was, please say this prayer below. All you need to do is confess Christ as King and Lord. And in the heavenly realm your name will be written in the Lamb's book of life. All the soldiers in the army of God are listed in that great book. Speak this prayer with your entire heart, dear one, and get ready to be transformed!

Lord Jesus, you are the Prince who comes to rescue the broken, the One who came to set me free. Please, Lord, come into my life today and rescue me from all my darkness, from all my shame. Forgive me for running to the arms of this world rather than the arms of a Savior. Holy Spirit, come into my life, restore me, and bind up my wounds. I am a great sinner and I am desperate for you. Take hold of me as I take hold of you right now at this very moment. Take my heart, Jesus, and make it like yours. Transform me from the inside out. Take my life today and use it forevermore for your kingdom. I am yours and you are mine. Live in me, Jesus! Today I make this covenant with you. I am your daughter/son and today you have become my Father and my Prince. Thank you, Lord, that my name is now written in the Lamb's book of life! May I never be the same, and may I be a mighty soldier for my generations to come. Amen.

Praise God, you were just commissioned and set apart as His very own soldier in the army of God! I pray that you serve Him bravely and set captives free! You have a new identity, dear warrior. Now walk in it and be ready for the call to arms!

CHAPTER 22

A Call to Arms

*A*s soldiers, we must dedicate our lives to serve our King and take hold of the Enemy, the great abductor of Christ's children. I want you to join me in this war. Will you run this race with me? Will you war with me? Will you decide today to stand up for yourself, your family, and generations to come? Maybe you and your family can have a different beginning than mine.

Dear soldier, consider this Scripture. "Don't you know that in a race all the runners compete, but only one wins the prize? So then, run to win! Now every athlete in training submits himself to strict discipline, and he does it just to win a laurel wreath that will soon wither away. But we do it to win a crown that will last forever. I don't run aimlessly but straight for the finish line; I don't shadow-box but try to make every punch count" (1 Cor. 9:24-27).

As you read, we do not battle for a withered laurel wreath; we battle for the crown of glory, one that will never wither! This passage encourages us not just to run the race but to win it! Not just to go to battle but to win the battle! Go for the crown that will last forever! And as for shadow boxing, punch something, would you? Punch Satan for what he has done, and knock him down for what he plans on doing to your generations to come!

In Christ, we were raised from the dead, not to act dead but to war with purpose! I don't know about you, but in my house, the war is on. No more will Satan have comfort and entertainment in my house. "As for me and my house we will serve the Lord" (Josh 24:15). And while I am quoting Joshua, may I remind you that God has called you out to the battlefield? Just as God spoke to Joshua, He speaks to you now, saying, "Dear son and daughter, be strong and courageous, for I the Lord your God go with you wherever you may go!" (Josh 1:9). Are you ready to go? If he goes with us, what shall we fear?

Ambassadors of Christ, it is time to drive the Enemy from our ground, the ground that Christ Jesus purchased for us on the cross! I pray that this book has inspired you enough to say, "No more, Satan! You will not have my family; you will not have my generations to come." It is time to stand up to this giant intruder. As King David said, "You come against me with a sword and spear, but I come after you in the name of the Lord my God and I will defeat you!" (1 Sam. 17:45). And what did King David do when the giant went down? He cut off his head! What are you waiting for? Go and cut off the Enemy's head with God's Son and His Word!

Broken, the Enemy had you, and yes, broken you were, but today you can be broken no more! I am broken no more because He is broken no more. I am because He is! What will you be?

CHAPTER 23

Broken No More Session

We are human, but we don't
wage war as humans do.

—2 Cor. 10:3

I want to share with you how God has blessed me with a counseling ministry called Broken No More. He is using my life to help set captives free. My test became a testimony, and my mess a message. What is so mind-boggling is the fact that I barely made it through high school and I'm perplexed that I completed grad school! It had to be God at work! And can you believe that He would trust me to run a ministry? After all you have just read, you must be asking the same question! Why this one, God?

If you have recovered from your shock, I believe we should have at least one Broken No More counseling session to discuss warring. My style is biblically bold and firm, but spoken in love. I want to make our first session together about marriage and family. Why? Because Satan brutally attacks the home.

Let us talk about Satan for a moment. The spiritual realm is as real as you are, as real as the book you are holding, and demons are real—thus the need war against them. Most of my clients have seen them, and all have experienced spiritual attacks.

So I get it Maryann, but now what? Well, let me speak to parents for a moment. If you are not standing guard in your home and using Christ's Word as a weapon against principalities and rulers of the dark, it is the same as if you watched a psychopath walk into your home, grab your children, and viciously and brutally attack them. In the natural world, what would you do if you saw this happen? They are screaming for help! "Help, Daddy, this hurts." "Help, Mommy. I am scared." "Will you protect us, Daddy?" Good parents would fight to protect their children. You would battle the intruder and maybe even try to kill him.

When you refuse to pick up the Word of God and use it as a weapon in the spiritual realm, you are a doormat for Satan and you are permitting him to use your children for target practice. A great way to use the Word as a weapon is to set up a "war box." I often ask my clients to go home and write out warfare Scripture verses on index cards and keep them in a little box. And when the war is on, grab that war box and begin to speak the Word of God over your family and the circumstance. Speaking and believing the Word bring forth power. Let me share an example.

A few months ago, my kids ran into our master bedroom filled with fear. As a warfare counselor, I believe wholeheartedly in using God's Word for power and to make Satan flee. The Bible trains us for war. The Word says, "We battle not against flesh and blood but against powers and rulers of the unseen world" (Eph. 6:12). I knew on this night that my children were being tormented, and since I had to fulfill a speaking engagement the next day, I also knew that the enemy wanted my mind and my rest. So as the kids shared all their fears, I did what I am trained to do: I quoted Scripture. "God has not given us the spirit of fear but of power, love, and sound mind" (2 Tim. 1:7).

I closed my eyes to go back to sleep, but instead I saw a pop-up in my mind of the spirit of fear. The vision startled me to the core. I saw a dreadful, chalk-colored demon whose teeth were chattering. The face was deformed and horrendous. The vision disturbed me greatly, and I said in a bold, loud voice, "My God has not given us a spirit of fear, but of power, love, and sound mind!" Finally, we all drifted off to a peaceful sleep.

The next morning I was refreshed and ready for the day's tasks. One was homeschooling. After breakfast, as Ashley began her math assignment, she stopped what she was doing, glanced up at me, and said, "Mom, I forgot to tell you what I saw last night in our room." I put my book down, gave her my full attention, and asked, "What did you see?" I had already forgotten about our prayer and was busy preparing for my day. She said, "Well, last night I saw God's hand in our bedroom!" She said it was huge and bright! She said that God's hand had swept around our bed then came above us and stopped right beside her.

In complete amazement over my daughter's description of her vision, I asked, "Ashley, what did you do?" She said that the brightness of God's hand made her cry and she pulled the covers up to her nose, then watched as His hand faded away. I was in tears after she had shared her story. What a confirmation of the power we behold in Him and His Word!

Let us talk about our marriages and how to fight Satan. There are only two sides to take in the marital war; we can take Satan's side or God's. Typically, when couples come in battered and bruised, both have given up the fight for territory, meaning they have permitted Satan to move in and reside in their home and marriage.

How does this happen? Let us look at what occurs when one spouse does not war for one another. When you choose not to raise your sword and join a spouse in battle—the husband or wife struggling with addiction, lust, depression, or infidelity—you are now fighting that spouse, and whose side are you on?

You are fighting for the kingdom of light or the kingdom of darkness. Are you fighting for your marriage the way Christ so fought for you?

The Word says, "I command you this, that you love others as I have loved you" (John 13:34). The Word of God is a command, not an option! Are you fighting against your spouse, thus bringing glory to the kingdom of darkness? When you war like Satan and speak death into marriage, death is what will happen! But when you war with God by using His Word and speak life into your marriage, your marriage will live! Ask yourself, whose side am I fighting for?

In my own marriage, there was a time when I took sides with Satan. My husband fell into Satan's trap of pornography, and I joined sides with enemy forces and condemned him, ridiculed him, and questioned his faith. I listened to the Enemy and was used as a mouthpiece. I shot daggers at Michael. I turned on him rather than turning on the Enemy. Mike was already being condemned by the Evil One. What kind of warrior was I to turn on a man who was already bleeding?

Whose side are you on today? If we are to imitate Christ in marriage, we must remember that He warred for us, even when we were not worthy. Thank God He did not turn against us. We need to fight for our marriages as Christ fought for us.

The next area to address in marriage counseling is "look out for me only" syndrome. We are not on this earth for "me." We are here for Him. Our King commissioned us to battle for Him, not us. And that means getting your marriage in order so you and your spouse can war for a greater purpose. It is not about you! Christ did not come to save marriage. He came to save people. When are we going to stand up and drive Satan from our marriages, our children, and our grounds so that we can get to work for the kingdom?

Marriage is great for couples, but I believe God ordained marriage for the war we are to fight in unity. Satan is a distracter; he would much rather have you war against one another and be so exhausted from the fight that you are too distracted to see the pain of your children and too distracted to see that the Enemy is tormenting them and destroying your legacy. If you remain distracted, that will keep you preoccupied and too busy for the kingdom's work.

You may say, "Great, Maryann. I get it. But how do I get my marriage back in order so we can fight the Enemy?" There is only one way, and that is getting your marriage to Christ in order. A vital question to address is what your relationship with Christ looks like. I use a scale from zero through ten. Zero represents a dead relationship with the Lord, and a ten is an intimate walk with Christ, reading His word and walking in obedience. Most of the couples I see admit that they are a three or a four.

I ask them to look at the scale again. "Where would you fall on this scale in the area of marital satisfaction?" It's no surprise that the number is the same, a three or a four. Simply put, when husband and wife invest in their marriage to the Lord, bringing their number to an eight or a ten, naturally their marital satisfaction improves as well.

Is the number in your relationship with Christ a three or a four? If so, that is about the same size as the weapon you use against Satan. If I am going to war, I want to use a weapon that rates a ten! In the spiritual realm, when we invest wholeheartedly in our marriage to Christ, our weapons are naturally a ten and so is our marital satisfaction. And the more we nourish our relationship with our God, the healthier our marriages become and the more potent we become to our enemies!

This approach will reap a great harvest. If you have been planting weeds in your marriage, it is time to plant seeds, and at harvest time you will have enough food to feed your family spiritually! Have your children been hungry for some fruit, Mom and Dad? Are they starving spiritually? If you grasp this concept, you will have a large enough harvest to feed the generations to come. If you don't, you will starve them. You decide.

This last session is for the men, the leaders in the home. God has made it clear to me that the men of the church are falling short of their God-given responsibilities. Over the past two-plus years, a common theme has emerged in my office in the area of marriage counseling: men are not leading their homes, children, and spouses and are failing to war for their families. The overwhelming number of complaints in counseling involve women pleading for their husbands to lead. They are overwhelmed with the responsibility of having to fill all the roles.

You know that song "Where Have All the Cowboys Gone?" Where have all the men of God gone? Where is John Wayne? What are we teaching our children when the men are sending the women into the battlefield against the Enemy while they are home heavily sedated by the things of this world? You men of God need to fight the battle with a sword, not a remote control, a iPhone, or iPad. The situation must change, and husbands must be awakened from sedation before the Enemy consumes their entire bloodlines. Women are worn out and tired of fighting solo. This war must be fought in unity as one flesh in power, but instead the Enemy has couples warring against each other in marriage. What a brilliant tactic.

God did not raise His sons to be cowards, with husbands sending their women and children into battle. God raised His sons to *war*, but Satan is stealing this desire from their hearts. There is a war hero inside of every man, and that includes you. Wives are desperately waiting for those heroes to stand up and fight for their families and generations to come. You have a sword, guys. Use it.

In closing, my desire is for you to put this book down and pick up a sword, God's sword. This book is evidence that we need a call to arms! Brothers and sisters, the war is on. Now let us take back the ground that Satan is standing on. It belongs to us! I am passionate about fighting the fight. Christ is our King and we are His ambassadors. Let us not be just any soldiers, but soldiers who are valiant. Christ is worth our efforts! And we should feel honored and privileged that He would chose to commission us!

Be a hero in your home, and if you want to know how to be the greatest and bravest war hero, seek Jesus because there has never been a greater example of a war hero in all of history! You possess His character. Now walk in it. May God use you and may He bless you and your generations to come. As for you, Satan, we are coming against you with a sword like no other. We are coming to restore what you have plundered. The battle is on, and in the name of Jesus, Lord of Heaven's Army, we have already won! Broken no more!

ABOUT THE AUTHOR

*M*aryann McMellon is the founder and president of BrokenNoMore Counseling Inc., a counseling practice that inspires families to war against Satan using God's Word as a weapon to break free from generational sin and bondage. She is a counselor, speaker, and author. Maryann is a graduate of Liberty University and holds a master's degree with a specialization in marriage and family counseling. She is married to Michael McMellon, an officer in the United States Air Force. Maryann and Michael are the blessed parents of two homeschooled children, Ashley and Jacob, the joy of their lives and future warriors for Christ. They reside in Northern Virginia.